LIVING IN HIS GRACE
A QUEST TOWARDS A CHRIST-CENTERED LIFE

STEVEN WOODS
RANDALL JOHNSON

LIVING IN HIS GRACE

A QUEST TOWARDS A CHRIST CENTERED LIFE

Steven Woods & Randall Johnson
DiscipleshipPublishing.com
or
https://www.ilncenter.com/publishing/

Edited By: Becki L. Zilliox

ISBN: 978-1-945423-53-3

CONTENTS

FORWARD

Welcome to *Living in His Grace, A Quest Towards A Christ-Centered Life.* We are delighted to embark on this transformative journey with you as we explore the depths of healthy Christian living through the lens of God's Word. Our goal is simple: to let the Bible speak and encourage you with its wisdom on living a life centered on God.

In a world filled with countless philosophies and self-help approaches, it is easy to lose sight of what truly matters in our Christian walk. Our desire is to provide you with a guide—a roadmap that leads you to a place where God's grace abounds, where faith flourishes, and where love, integrity, and gratitude become the defining qualities of your life.

Throughout this book, we have meticulously crafted each chapter to delve into vital aspects of Christian living. From faith, prayer, and love to compassion, integrity, and stewardship, we cover a wide range of topics essential to nurturing a Christ-centered life. Each chapter is grounded in the timeless truths of the Bible, offering profound insights and practical guidance for your personal journey.

We want to emphasize that this book is not about our own opinions or perspectives. Instead, it is an exploration of what the Bible teaches about healthy Christian living. Our aim is to let God's Word take center stage, shining light on the path that leads to a life lived in His grace.

As you engage with the chapters ahead, we encourage you to approach them with an open heart and a receptive spirit. Reflect on the biblical truths presented, allowing them to penetrate your thoughts, attitudes, and actions. Consider how you can apply these truths to your daily life and allow them to shape your character, relationships, and purpose.

It is our sincerest hope that "Living in His Grace" serves as a blessing and a helpful companion on your journey. May it provide you with insights, encouragement, and inspiration to navigate the complexities of life with grace and wisdom. May it deepen your understanding of God's love and ignite a passionate pursuit of a Christ-centered existence.

We are honored to walk alongside you in this quest towards a life centered on God. May His grace abound in your heart and His Word be a lamp unto your feet. Together, let us seek to live in the fullness of His love, as we embrace the transformative power of His Word.

Blessings on your journey,

Randall Johnson and Steven Woods

CHAPTER 1

THE CHRISTIAN LIFE

Hello there, and welcome on this exciting journey! We're about to embark on an exploration of what it truly means to live a Christian life, especially from the perspective of a young person like yourself. I'm thrilled that you're here, and I pray that the words on these pages will inspire, challenge, and guide you as you cultivate a deeper relationship with God.

At the heart of the Christian life is a vibrant, personal relationship with God. It's not just about following a set of rules or traditions but about knowing God personally and walking with Him daily. Jesus, Himself, said, *"This is eternal life: that they may know you, the only true God, and Jesus Christ, whom you have sent."* (John 17:3). As we journey together through this book, we'll learn more about how to nurture this all-important relationship.

Next, let's talk about our ultimate role model: Jesus Christ. He lived a perfect life of love, kindness, and obedience to God. As we dive deeper into His teachings and actions in subsequent chapters, we'll discover practical ways we can strive to live like Him and reflect His character in our daily lives. As 1 Peter 2:21 says, *"Christ suffered for you, leaving you an example, that you should follow in his steps."*

Living the Christian life also involves adhering to key principles that Jesus taught, such as love, forgiveness, service, integrity, and many more. We'll unpack each of these in the chapters ahead, exploring how they can transform our lives and relationships.

Another crucial element of the Christian life is the Holy Spirit. When Jesus left earth, He didn't leave us alone. He sent the Holy Spirit to guide, empower, and transform us. As we'll discover, the Holy Spirit is a constant companion and helper in our journey of faith (John 14:16).

Part of cultivating a relationship with God involves practicing spiritual disciplines like prayer, Bible study, worship, fasting, and fellowship. These are like exercises for our spiritual health, helping us grow closer to God and stronger in our faith. We'll explore these in-depth in the coming chapters.

Community plays a big role too. God designed us to live in relationship with others, supporting and encouraging one another in our faith journeys. As Hebrews 10:24-25 reminds us, *"And let us consider how we may spur one another on toward love and good deeds, not giving up meeting together...but encouraging one another."* This is God's built in system for accountability of which we all are in need if we want to become more like Christ. (Galatians 6:1; Matthew 18:15).

It's important to acknowledge that being a Christian isn't always easy. We face unique challenges and pressures in today's world. But remember, God promises to be with us every step of the way, providing guidance and strength

(Joshua 1:9). We'll talk more about navigating these challenges in later chapters.

Finally, it's important to know that this book isn't just a collection of our thoughts. It's a reflection of our own journey with God. We've experienced firsthand the joys and challenges of living a Christian life, and we're excited to share what we've learned along the way.

So that's a brief overview of what we'll be exploring in this book. Each chapter will delve deeper into these areas, providing practical advice, biblical insights, and real-life examples to guide and inspire you. I pray that this journey will bring you closer to God and help you live out your faith in meaningful and impactful ways. So, are you ready? Let's dive in!

Chapter 2

Faith

In this chapter, we'll uncover what faith really means, how it shapes our relationship with God and Jesus, its role in our salvation, and how it manifests itself in everyday life.

What is Faith?

At its core, faith is more than just belief—it's complete trust in God's promises, even when we can't see them. The Bible defines faith in Hebrews 11:1 as *"confidence in what we hope for and assurance about what we do not see."* It's a confident trust in Christ that guides our thoughts, our actions, and our everyday relationship with God.

Jesus as the Object of Our Faith

Faith is not just about believing in a higher power—it's about trusting in Jesus Christ. He is the Son of God, our Savior, and the perfect expression of God's love for us. Jesus himself said in John 14:1, *"Do not let your hearts be troubled. You believe in God; believe also in me."* When we place our faith in Jesus, we're receiving His love, His sacrifice, His forgiveness, and His guidance for our lives. Our acceptance is not based on what we have done but upon His work and what He has done.

FAITH AND SALVATION

Our faith is essential for our salvation. It's through faith that we receive the gift of God's grace. As Ephesians 2:8-9 tells us, *"For it is by grace you have been saved, through faith—and this is not from yourselves, it is the gift of God, not by works, so that no one can boast."* Faith isn't about earning God's love—it's about trusting in God's Son thereby receiving His gift of salvation.

Faith is our response to the Good News of the Gospel. It is supernatural in the sense that it comes from God, and it is natural in the sense that we believe in Christ in response to the message preached. This is how we receive forgiveness, cleansing, and freedom from sin. God gives us grace to trust in Christ, and therefore, we become His children.

LIVING BY FAITH

Faith is also about living out our trust in God in our daily lives. It influences our decisions, our actions, and how we interact with others. The Bible is filled with stories of individuals who lived by faith. Remember Abraham? He didn't know where he was going, but he trusted God and stepped out in faith (Hebrews 11:8). We are called to live by faith too, as 2 Corinthians 5:7 says, *"For we live by faith, not by sight."* Genuine faith is demonstrated in obedience to God's commands. When one trusts in Christ and begins to walk with Him, they will desire to obey Him, delight in His ways, and love others.

GROWING YOUR FAITH

Just like a seed, our faith needs to be nurtured to grow. Faith does not grow on its own, just as a baby does not grow on its own. The baby needs to be given proper nutrition in order to grow, and the same applies to faith. We grow in faith through prayer, fasting, studying the Bible, fellowship with other believers, and obeying God's commands. These disciplines draw us closer to God and help us understand His will, which, in turn, strengthens our faith.

FAITH IN TIMES OF DOUBT

It's natural to experience doubt or uncertainty at times. But even in those moments, we can turn to God in faith. Consider the father in Mark 9:24 who exclaimed, *"I do believe; help me overcome my unbelief!"* Doubt doesn't have to be the end of faith—it can be a starting point for deeper trust in God.

Uncertainty, however, can happen for various reasons, but one particular reason worth noting is sin. Our sin can cause us to become uncertain about our standing before God, to doubt our acceptance, and to question whether or not we are genuinely a Christian or not. These thoughts are normal and should be explored through the lens of scripture, a godly mentor, a pastor, or a Christian friend. We must be careful to avoid delving into despair because of being uncertain about the sincerity of our faith.

FAITH AND HOPE

Faith and hope are two sides of the same coin. Our faith in God gives us hope for the future, and that hope, in turn, strengthens our faith. As we've seen, faith is "confidence in what we hope for and assurance about what we do not see."

It's a forward-looking trust in God's promises and His plan for our lives.

We've taken a deep dive into the concept of faith - exploring its definition, its role in understanding God's nature, its centrality in our belief in Jesus, and its importance in our salvation. We've talked about what it means to live by faith, how to grow our faith, how to maintain it in times of doubt, and how it has a close relationship with hope.

As we wrap up this chapter, we want to encourage you to keep exploring, keep asking questions, and keep nurturing your faith. Faith isn't a one-time decision, instead it is but a journey that continues throughout our lives. Remember, even when you have questions or doubts, God is always there, ready to meet you where you are.

We hope that this exploration of faith has been helpful to you, and we pray that it will deepen your relationship with God. As we move on to the next chapter, we'll be discussing another foundational aspect of the Christian life: Prayer. Until then, keep growing in your faith, and remember, you are loved by a faithful God!

Faith is more than just a belief—it's a whole-hearted trust in Christ. It is a trust that abandons self and any other reliance on external things like relationships, materialism, success, works, or any thing that would try to compete with Christ. Like any relationship, it requires time, commitment, and love, but the rewards of a faith-filled life are beyond anything we can imagine. So, keep seeking, keep trusting, and keep growing in your faith. God is with you every step of the way, and He promises He will never leave you alone. He will walk with you, in you, and move upon you.

CHAPTER 3

PRAYER

Prayer is a vital aspect of the Christian faith, serving as a means of communication between believers and God. From a biblical perspective, prayer is not primarily about changing God's mind or persuading Him to act in a certain way. Instead, prayer is intended to transform and align our hearts and minds with God's will. Through prayer, we develop a deeper relationship with God and allow Him to shape us according to His purposes.

One key passage that highlights the purpose of prayer is found in the Gospel of Matthew, where Jesus teaches His disciples about prayer. In Matthew 6:9-13, Jesus provides a model prayer, commonly known as the Lord's Prayer. This prayer emphasizes the acknowledgement of God's holiness, the submission to His will, and the request for daily provision, forgiveness, and protection. It demonstrates that prayer is a means of aligning our hearts and desires with God's agenda, rather than trying to manipulate or change God.

Another important passage that emphasizes the transformative aspect of prayer is found in the book of James.

James 4:3 states, *"When you ask, you do not receive, because you ask with wrong motives, that you may spend what you get on your pleasures."* This verse reminds us that prayer is not a tool for self-centered desires but an opportunity to seek God's will and align our motives with His. It teaches us to approach prayer with humility and surrender to God's plan rather than try to impose our own desires upon Him.

Furthermore, the apostle Paul provides insight into the purpose of prayer in his letter to the Philippians. In Philippians 4:6-7, Paul encourages believers, saying, *"Do not be anxious about anything, but in every situation, by prayer and petition, with thanksgiving, present your requests to God. And the peace of God, which transcends all understanding, will guard your hearts and your minds in Christ Jesus."* Here, prayer is depicted as a means to find peace and comfort in God's presence, allowing Him to transform our anxious hearts and minds into a state of trust and serenity.

WHAT IS PRAYER?

Prayer, from a Christian perspective, is our direct line of communication with God. It's a heart-to-heart, intimate conversation with the Creator of the universe. In scripture, we see Jesus praying not to change the Father's Will but to align Himself with the Father's Will (Luke 22:42).

THE POWER OF PRAYER

Prayer isn't just powerful—it's transformative. It can change circumstances, yes, but more importantly, it changes us. James 5:16 tells us *"The prayer of a righteous person is powerful and effective."* [Remember, our prayers touch the heart of God, and that's where their power lies.]

JESUS AND PRAYER

Our Savior, Jesus, provides us with the perfect model of prayer. He regularly withdrew from crowds and even His closest disciples to spend time in prayer, as we see in Luke 5:16: *"But Jesus often withdrew to lonely places and prayed."* Jesus prayed in times of thanksgiving, in times of decision, in times of distress, and He even prayed for His disciples and all believers.

DIFFERENT TYPES OF PRAYER

There are several forms of prayer, each important in its own way. We have prayers of praise, expressing our awe and love for God; prayers of petition, where we ask God for our needs; prayers of intercession, where we pray for others; prayers of confession, where we acknowledge our sins; and prayers of thanksgiving, where we express our gratitude to God. All of these forms help us communicate with God in different ways. Throughout the Bible, scripture guides us in these prayers.

PRAYER AND RELATIONSHIP WITH GOD

Prayer isn't just a religious duty—it's a relationship builder. Through prayer, we deepen our relationship with God, coming to understand His heart more fully. Jeremiah 29:12 tells us, *"Then you will call on me and come and pray to me, and I will listen to you."* Prayer is our invitation to know God more intimately.

PRACTICAL GUIDANCE ON HOW TO PRAY

Wondering how to pray? You're not alone. The disciples asked Jesus the same question, and His response gave us the Lord's Prayer (Matthew 6:9-13). This prayer serves as a template, guiding us in how to address God, seek His will, ask for our needs, seek forgiveness, and resist temptation.

OVERCOMING OBSTACLES IN PRAYER

Like any journey, the journey of prayer can have its obstacles—annoying distractions, feelings of distance, even nagging doubts, but Romans 8:26 reminds us, *"In the same way, the Spirit helps us in our weakness. We do not know what we ought to pray for, but the Spirit himself intercedes for us through wordless groans."* You're not alone in your prayer journey; God's Spirit is with you, helping you.

There we have it: a brief journey through the world of prayer. Remember, prayer is your personal conversation with God, and He's always ready to listen. I encourage you to make prayer a consistent part of your life, as you continue to grow in your faith.

Prayer is more than just a practice—it's a lifestyle. It's an ongoing dialogue with God, an opportunity to draw closer to Him every moment of every day. It's not just about asking for what we need, but it's building a relationship with our Creator, getting to know His heart, and aligning ourselves with His will.

Prayer is not just for the 'holy' moments—it's for the everyday moments, too. It's for the moments in the mornings when you're just waking up, for the moments when you're commuting or doing chores, for the moments when you are full of joy, and for the moments when you are in pain. God wants to share in all aspects of your life, not just the Sunday service or Bible study moments.

As we close this chapter, We want to encourage you to make prayer a priority in your life. Let it be the first thing you do in the morning and the last thing you do at night. Let it be your response to joy and your refuge in hardship. Remember, there's no 'right' way to pray—just pour out your heart to God, and He will hear you.

Keep praying, keep trusting, and keep growing in your faith. The journey is so worth it. God is with you every step of the way!

CHAPTER 4

LOVE & FORGIVENESS

L ove is the foundation of God's relationship with humanity, and forgiveness is the expression of that love. God's love for us is demonstrated through the sacrifice of Jesus, and our response to that love is to extend forgiveness to others. Love motivates forgiveness, and forgiveness is an act of love that seeks reconciliation and restoration. As followers of Christ, we are called to love one another and to extend forgiveness as a reflection of the love and forgiveness we have received from God.

WHAT IS LOVE?

Love is a word we hear often, but what does it really mean, especially from a Christian perspective?

In the Bible, love is considered the highest virtue, the greatest command, and the defining characteristic of a follower of Christ. It's more than a feeling—it's an action, a commitment, and a way of life. *"Love is patient, love is kind. It does not envy, it does not boast, it is not proud. It does not dishonor others, it is not self-seeking, it is not easily angered, it keeps no record of wrongs"* (1 Corinthians 13:4-7).

In its purest form, love is selfless and unconditional, mirroring the love that God has for each of us. It's about caring for others' well-being as much as our own, and it's about showing compassion, grace, and kindness in all circumstances.

THE GREATEST COMMANDMENT

Jesus Himself gave us the greatest commandment, a dual directive that centers on love. In Matthew 22:37-39, Jesus says, *"Love the Lord your God with all your heart and with all your soul and with all your mind. This is the first and greatest commandment. And the second is like it: 'Love your neighbor as yourself."*

Let's break this down a bit. Loving God with all our heart, soul, and mind involves dedicating every part of our being to Him. It means seeking Him first, honoring Him in our actions, and pursuing a relationship with Him above all else.

Loving our neighbors as ourselves isn't always easy, but it's equally important. It means treating others with kindness and respect, helping those in need, and forgiving those who hurt us. It's about recognizing the inherent value in every person, just as God does.

GOD'S LOVE FOR US

Now, why are we commanded to love like this? Because that's how God loves us—unconditionally, selflessly, and completely.

John 3:16, one of the most well-known verses in the Bible, says, *"For God so loved the world that He gave His one and only Son, that whoever believes in Him shall not perish but have eternal life."*

God's love for us is so profound that He made the ultimate sacrifice, allowing us to be reconciled to Him.

God's love isn't dependent on our performance. It doesn't fluctuate based on our successes or failures. Instead, it's constant, unwavering, and freely given. We don't have to earn God's love; we simply have to accept it.

LOVING OTHERS

How, then, can we love others as ourselves? First, we must understand that this command goes beyond just treating others with kindness. It involves a deep, selfless concern for their well-being, mirroring the love that God has for us.

Jesus, Himself, gave us the ultimate example of how to love others. He healed the sick, comforted the sorrowful, and even washed the feet of His disciples, a task typically reserved for servants. He showed love not just in big, monumental actions, but in everyday interactions.

Applying this to our lives means being patient with others, just as God is patient with us. It means forgiving those who have wronged us, helping those in need, and seeking to understand before being understood. It may not be easy, but remember, *"With man this is impossible, but with God all things are possible"* (Matthew 19:26).

WHAT IS FORGIVENESS?

In the Christian context, forgiveness is the act of pardoning an offense and letting go of resentment. It's not about ignoring the wrong or pretending it didn't hurt. Instead, it's about choosing to release the hold that the hurt has on us.

Why is forgiveness so important? Colossians 3:13 says, *"Bear with each other and forgive one another if any of you has a grievance against someone. Forgive as the Lord forgave you."* Forgiveness frees us from the bonds of anger and resentment, and it reflects the forgiveness that God has graciously extended to us. Forgiveness is one of the clearest manifestations of Christ's love that a Christian can display in the World.

GOD'S FORGIVENESS OF OUR SINS

To truly understand forgiveness, we must first grasp the immensity of God's forgiveness towards us. We must understand the gravity of our sin against God in order to appreciate what He did through His Son. Through Jesus Christ's sacrificial death on the cross, God has forgiven all our sins—past, present, and future. He treated Christ as though He was us, and in turn treated us as though we were His Son. In other words, when we repent and receive God's forgiveness, Christ's sacrifice becomes personal. It is applied to us. When Christ went to the cross, He took the punishment for your sin. Christ became your substitute, He took your sin and He gave you His righteousness because of His love for you.

The Apostle John writes, *"If we confess our sins, He is faithful and just and will forgive us our sins and purify us from all unrighteousness"* (1 John 1:9). This verse assures us that no sin is too great for God's forgiveness. When we confess and turn away from our sins, God is faithful to forgive us and cleanse us.

God's forgiveness is complete and absolute. He doesn't hold our past mistakes against us. Instead, He forgives and forgets, removing our sins as far as the east is from the west (Psalm 103:12).

One of the greatest challenges we as Christians face is to learn how we can extend this same kind of forgiveness to others. It's a challenging journey, but with God's help, we can learn to forgive as we have been forgiven.

FORGIVING OTHERS

It is not easy to forgive those who have wronged us. When we are hurt by others, our natural inclination might be to hold onto anger, resentment, or even seek revenge. However, Jesus calls us to a different path - one of forgiveness.

In Matthew 18:21-22, Peter asked Jesus how many times he should forgive someone who sins against him. *"Seven times?"*, he proposed. But Jesus answered, *"Not seven times, but seventy-seven times."* This doesn't mean we stop forgiving on the four hundred-ninetieth time, but rather, Jesus is highlighting the limitless nature of forgiveness.

Forgiving others isn't about ignoring the wrong or saying that it was acceptable. It's about releasing the hold that anger and resentment can have on us. It's about choosing to reflect God's mercy and grace, even when it's hard.

Practically, this might mean having a conversation with someone who has hurt you, expressing your feelings, and then choosing to let go of the resentment. It could also mean praying for that person and asking God to help you forgive them in your heart, even if you can't reconcile with them in person.

Forgiveness is a journey, not a destination. It takes time and it's okay to progress at your own pace. The important thing is that you're moving forward, not staying stuck in resentment.

LOVE AND FORGIVENESS IN ACTION

Let's look at some examples of love and forgiveness in action.

Consider the story of the Prodigal Son (Luke 15:11-32). Despite his son's disrespect and reckless living, the father welcomes him home with open arms, full of love and forgiveness. He doesn't hold his son's past against him but, instead, celebrates his return. This story paints a vivid picture of God's love and forgiveness towards us.

In another instance, Jesus shows love to a woman caught in adultery (John 8:1-11). The crowd wanted to stone her, but Jesus responded with forgiveness, saying, *"Let any one of you who is without sin be the first to throw a stone at her."* After the crowd disperses, Jesus tells the woman, *"Neither do I condemn you. Go now and leave your life of sin."* Here, Jesus demonstrates love and forgiveness while also encouraging a transformed life.

These stories remind us that love and forgiveness aren't abstract concepts. They have real, tangible impacts on our lives and the lives of those around us. As we continue this journey together, let's strive to make love and forgiveness the cornerstones of our interactions with others.

As we wrap up this chapter, we hope you have a deeper understanding of what love and forgiveness mean in the Christian context, and how you can actively practice these principles in your daily life. Remember, love and forgiveness aren't just actions—they're a reflection of God's character in us. Pray and ask God for the grace to forgive others, and He will do just that; so let's grow in love, forgiveness, and understanding.

CHAPTER 5

COMPASSION & SERVICE

Compassion is the deep, heartfelt response to the suffering and needs of others. It is rooted in love and empathy, compelling believers to reach out and alleviate the pain and struggles of those around them. Compassion is not merely a fleeting emotion but a call to action, reflecting the character of God Himself. In numerous passages, the Bible highlights God's compassionate nature, describing Him as *"gracious and merciful, slow to anger and abounding in steadfast love"* (Psalm 145:8). Similarly, service is the practical outpouring of compassion, as believers selflessly dedicate themselves to meeting the physical, emotional, and spiritual needs of others. Jesus, in His earthly ministry, exemplified service by washing the feet of His disciples and ultimately laying down His life for the salvation of humanity. As followers of Christ, we are called to imitate His example and serve others wholeheartedly, as expressed in Galatians 5:13, *"You, my brothers and sisters, were called to be free. But do not use your freedom to indulge the flesh; rather, serve one another humbly in love."* In essence, biblical compassion and service are intertwined, compelling believers to extend love, mercy, and practical assistance to those in need, reflecting the selfless and sacrificial nature of Christ.

UNDERSTANDING COMPASSION

Compassion, in its simplest form, is the feeling of empathy towards those who are suffering, coupled with a desire to alleviate their pain. From a Christian perspective, it extends beyond mere sympathy to active love in action. Compassion isn't just about feeling sorry for someone; it's about stepping into their shoes, understanding their struggles, and doing what we can to help.

This virtue is deeply rooted in the Bible. In Colossians 3:12, Paul writes, *"Therefore, as God's chosen people, holy and dearly loved, clothe yourselves with compassion, kindness, humility, gentleness and patience."* As followers of Christ, we're not only recipients of God's compassion but also channels through which His compassion flows to others.

Jesus, Himself, was the embodiment of compassion. He healed the sick, fed the hungry, and comforted the brokenhearted. His compassion wasn't selective; He extended it to all, regardless of their social status, ethnicity, or past. One of the most touching instances is when Jesus, moved with compassion, touched and healed a leper, a person considered unclean and outcast by society (Mark 1:40-41).

UNDERSTANDING SERVICE

Service, from a Christian standpoint, is the selfless act of helping and serving others, often at the cost of personal comfort or gain. It's Christ's love in action through us, expressed through the use of our time, talents, and resources.

The Bible places a high value on service. In Mark 10:45, Jesus says, *"For even the Son of Man did not come to be served, but to serve, and to give His life as a ransom for many."* Jesus, though He was God, took on the humble position of a servant. He washed His disciples' feet, a task typically done by the lowest of servants, demonstrating that no act of service is beneath us when done out of love (John 13:1-17).

THE INTERSECTION OF COMPASSION AND SERVICE

Compassion and service are two sides of the same coin. Compassion stirs within us a deep empathy for others in their suffering, while service is the outward expression of this compassion.

James, in his epistle, emphasizes the futility of faith without deeds, saying, *"Suppose a brother or a sister is without clothes and daily food. If one of you says to them, 'Go in peace; keep warm and well fed,' but does nothing about their physical needs, what good is it?"* (James 2:15-16).

In essence, our compassion should drive us to action, to serve those around us. It's one thing to feel for the poor, the sick, the lonely, and another to do something about it. As we progress in this chapter, we'll explore practical ways to express our compassion through service, following in the footsteps of Jesus, the perfect exemplar of compassion and service.

PRACTICAL WAYS TO SHOW COMPASSION

Now that we understand what compassion is, how can we show it in our daily lives? Remember, compassion isn't about grand gestures; often, it's the small acts of kindness that make a significant impact.

Listening: Sometimes, the most compassionate thing we can do is simply to listen. When someone shares their struggles, listen intently. Show them that you care and that they're not alone.

Comforting: Reach out to those who are hurting. A comforting word, a prayer, or even a silent hug can mean a lot to someone going through a difficult time.

Helping: Look for opportunities to help. It could be as simple as helping an elderly neighbor with their groceries or volunteering at a local charity.

In the Bible, we see numerous examples of compassion in action. The Good Samaritan (Luke 10:25-37), for instance, didn't just feel pity for the injured man on the road; he took practical steps to help. He bandaged his wounds, brought him to an inn, and paid for his stay. His compassion was active, not passive.

THE CALL TO SERVE

As Christians, we're called to serve others. Jesus said, *"Just as the Son of Man did not come to be served, but to serve..."* (Matthew 20:28). Serving others is not just about doing good deeds; it's a way of living that reflects our faith in action.

When Jesus washed His disciples' feet, Peter initially resisted. But Jesus replied, *"Unless I wash you, you have no part with me"* (John 13:8). Through this act, Jesus showed that service is not beneath anyone. If He, the Lord and Master, can serve, so should we.

Service is not just for others; it also changes us. It humbles us, shifts our focus from ourselves to others, and allows us to experience God's love in a profound way. As we serve others, we serve God.

PRACTICAL WAYS TO SERVE

Serving others doesn't always require a grand gesture or a title. The fact that you are a Christian is all you need to know in order to serve others. Here are some practical ways you can serve those around you:

Volunteering: Consider volunteering your time at a local charity, church, or community center.

Helping Neighbors: Look for ways to help your neighbors. It could be mowing a lawn, babysitting, or running errands for an elderly neighbor.

Mentoring: If you're particularly skilled in a certain area, consider mentoring someone who wants to learn. This could be in academics, arts, sports, or even spiritual matters.

Remember the parable of the sheep and goats in Matthew 25:31-46. Jesus said that whatever we do for the least of our brothers and sisters, we do for Him. When we serve others, especially those in need, we're serving Christ Himself.

COMPASSION, SERVICE, AND THE MODERN WORLD

In a world that often seems driven by self-interest, the virtues of compassion and service may seem old-fashioned or even irrelevant. Yet, as followers of Christ, we are called to swim against the tide and demonstrate these virtues in our lives. The world needs compassion and service now more than ever.

In today's digital age, we are more connected than ever before, yet loneliness, depression, and anxiety are on the rise. There's a deep hunger for genuine, compassionate human connection, and this is where we can step in. By showing compassion, we can bring a ray of hope into the lives of those around us.

Similarly, there's a great need for service. There are countless opportunities to serve others in our communities, from volunteering at local shelters, to helping a neighbor in need. In serving others, we not only meet their needs but also experience joy and fulfillment ourselves.

There are challenges, of course. Showing compassion and serving others requires sacrifice. It might mean giving up our time, resources, or comfort, but as we look to Jesus, who *"did not come to be served, but to serve, and to give His life as a ransom for many"* (Mark 10:45), we are inspired to follow His example.

In this chapter, we've explored the concepts of compassion and service, two fundamental aspects of a Christian life. We've looked at what the Bible teaches about these virtues and how Jesus embodied them in His life. We've also discussed practical ways to show compassion and serve others in our day-to-day lives. Whether you're a husband, wife, child, church member, or some other vocation, you can apply the things we discussed to your own personal situation.

As followers of Christ, we are not just called to believe in Him but also to reflect His character in our lives. There's no better way to do that than to practice compassion and service. As we move forward, let's strive to cultivate these virtues in our lives, remembering that *"we love because He first loved us"* (1 John 4:19).

CHAPTER 6

INTEGRITY

UNDERSTANDING INTEGRITY

What is integrity? The dictionary might define it as the quality of being honest and having strong moral principles. Yet, as Christians, our understanding of integrity goes beyond this.

In the Bible, the word integrity is often used interchangeably with "uprightness" or "righteousness". It involves being truthful, fair, and trustworthy in all our dealings. It's about aligning our actions with our beliefs and values. Most importantly, it's about living in a way that pleases God.

Consider Proverbs 10:9, *"Whoever walks in integrity walks securely, but whoever takes crooked paths will be found out."* This scripture shows us that integrity gives us security and confidence, because we have nothing to hide.

INTEGRITY AND GOD'S CHARACTER

As we seek to understand and live out integrity, it's essential to look at God's character. The Bible tells us that God is a God of integrity. He is faithful and true in all His ways.

In Numbers 23:19, we read, *"God is not a man, that He should lie, nor a son of man, that He should change His mind. Does He speak and then not act? Does He promise and not fulfill?"* This verse tells us that God is utterly reliable. He always keeps His promises and never goes back on His Word.

God's integrity means that we can trust Him completely. It gives us confidence in His promises and assurance in His faithfulness. As His followers, we are called to reflect His integrity in our own lives. People should be able to trust our promises, and we must hold true to our word. This is one way we can reflect the character of God in our lives.

Jesus is our perfect model of integrity. Let's explore the importance of integrity in our Christian walk, and provide practical steps to nurture integrity in our daily lives. We ought to model this in our Christian life so that others will have an example to follow.

JESUS AS THE PERFECT MODEL OF INTEGRITY

Now that we've looked at the meaning of integrity and how it is embedded in God's character, let's explore the life of Jesus, who is our perfect model of integrity. Jesus, God in human form, showed us how to live a life of absolute integrity.

One of the most striking examples of Jesus' integrity is His interaction with the Pharisees. Despite the Pharisees' high social status and religious authority, Jesus didn't hesitate to speak the truth to them. He called them out for their hypocrisy and legalism, showing that He valued genuine righteousness over outward appearances (Matthew 23:27-28).

In the wilderness, Jesus was tempted by Satan to take shortcuts to power and to test God's care for Him. Nevertheless, even when no one else was watching, Jesus maintained His integrity by rejecting these temptations and staying true to His mission (Matthew 4:1-11).

Jesus was consistently truthful, loving, and righteous, regardless of the circumstances He faced. His life shows us that integrity isn't about behaving correctly just when others are watching: it's about being consistent in our character at all times.

INTEGRITY IN THE BIBLE

Throughout the Bible we find inspiring examples of men and women who displayed remarkable integrity in various situations. Two such characters are Daniel and Joseph.

Daniel, while serving in the court of the Babylonian king, refused to compromise his faith, even when it meant being thrown into a den of lions (Daniel 6). His integrity was evident to everyone around him, including the king himself.

Joseph, after being sold into slavery by his own brothers, ended up in Egypt. There, he faced a severe test of his integrity when Potipar's wife tried to seduce him. However, Joseph chose to do what was right instead of what was easy, maintaining his integrity even when it led to unjust punishment (Genesis 39).

These stories remind us that integrity often requires courage and sacrifice. However, God honors and rewards those who choose to walk in integrity.

As we continue in this chapter, we will discuss how we can live with integrity in our daily lives, and how we can cultivate this virtue in practical ways. As Christ's followers, we're called to reflect His character in everything we do. Consequently, a life of integrity is a powerful testimony of our faith in Him.

LIVING WITH INTEGRITY

Living with integrity is not just about avoiding wrongdoing. It's about actively doing what is right in every situation, whether big or small. As Christians, our integrity is reflected in how we interact with others, how we handle our responsibilities, and even how we react when no one else is watching.

Ephesians 4:25 instructs us, *"Therefore each of you must put off falsehood and speak truthfully to your neighbor, for we are all members of one body."* This scripture highlights that honesty and truthfulness, key aspects of integrity, aren't optional for us as believers. In fact, they are commandments.

Within our relationships, this might mean keeping our promises, being reliable, and admitting when we're wrong. At work or school, it could involve doing our best even when we're not being supervised, acknowledging our mistakes, and not taking credit for others' work.

PRACTICAL WAYS TO CULTIVATE INTEGRITY

So, how can we cultivate integrity in our lives? Here are some practical steps:

Study God's Word: The Bible is our guidebook for living a life of integrity. By studying it, we can understand God's standards and learn how to apply them in our lives.

Pray for Guidance: Ask God to help you live a life of integrity. The Holy Spirit can guide you in making the right decisions, even when it's challenging.

Be Accountable: Have trusted friends or mentors who can help you stay on the right path. Accountability can strengthen our resolve to live with integrity.

Practice Honesty: Make it a habit to speak truthfully, even when it's inconvenient. Honesty is a fundamental aspect of integrity.

Keep Your Promises: If you commit to doing something, follow through. Keeping your word is a practical way to demonstrate integrity.

Integrity impacts our Christian witness and we need to know how to maintain integrity in times of temptation. This is not something that happens once and you receive the reward. Living with integrity is a lifelong process, but every step brings us closer to reflecting Christ in our lives.

INTEGRITY AS A CHRISTIAN WITNESS

Our integrity is not only beneficial for our personal and spiritual growth, but it also serves as a witness to those around us. When we consistently display honesty, trustworthiness, and ethical behavior, we demonstrate to others what it means to be a follower of Christ.

In Matthew 5:16, Jesus instructs us, *"In the same way, let your light shine before others, that they may see your good deeds and glorify your Father in heaven."* Our integrity is part of that light, and it can draw others to Christ.

Imagine a situation at work where you find a colleague's mistake that could easily be overlooked. If you choose to correct the error instead of taking advantage of it, you're showing integrity. People may notice your actions and recognize something different about you—something that reflects Christ.

MAINTAINING INTEGRITY IN TIMES OF TEMPTATION

Living with integrity isn't always easy. There will be times when we're tempted to compromise our values, perhaps to take the easy way out or to gain some temporary benefit.

In such moments, it's crucial to remember the example of Christ, who resisted temptation by leaning on God's word (Matthew 4:1-11). We can do the same by memorizing and meditating on scriptures about integrity, such as Proverbs 11:3: *"The integrity of the upright guides them, but the unfaithful are destroyed by their duplicity."*

When facing temptation, it's also helpful to pray for strength and guidance. God promises to provide a way out of every temptation (1 Corinthians 10:13), and He will help us stand firm if we turn to Him.

As we conclude this chapter, let's remember that integrity is more than just a moral virtue - it's a reflection of our identity in Christ. As followers of Jesus, we're called to live lives of honesty, reliability, and righteousness, even when no one is watching.

Living with integrity won't always be easy, but it's worth the effort. As we grow in integrity, we not only honor God but also impact those around us, demonstrating the transformative power of Christ's love.

CHAPTER 7

RESPECT

Respect is a key component in our daily life. We are to respect others, as well as ourselves, and in doing so, we honor God. The Bible says what we do to the least of God's children we have done as unto Christ (Matthew 25:40). How we treat each other is how we are treating Christ. This is why it is important to treat each other with respect, thereby respecting Christ.

UNDERSTANDING RESPECT

So, what is respect? At its core, respect is about recognizing and appreciating the worth and dignity of all God's creations. It's about seeing the image of God in ourselves and in others, regardless of our differences.

Biblically, respect is an essential part of how we are called to interact with the world. 1 Peter 2:17 sums it up well: *"Show proper respect to everyone, love the family of believers, fear God, honor the emperor."* This scripture not only commands us to respect everyone but also gives us a framework of the different forms of respect: respect for each other, for the community of believers, for God, and for authority.

Respect is an integral part of many biblical teachings, and it is interwoven with principles like love, kindness, and humility. As we delve deeper into this chapter, we'll see how respect is not merely an abstract concept but a guiding principle that shapes our actions, attitudes, and relationships.

RESPECT FOR ONESELF

Before we can genuinely respect others, we must first learn to respect ourselves. So what does self-respect look like from a Christian perspective?

Self-respect begins with understanding our intrinsic value as God's creation. Psalm 139:14 tells us, *"I praise you because I am fearfully and wonderfully made; your works are wonderful, I know that full well."* Recognizing that we are wonderfully made by God instills in us a sense of self-respect.

Nevertheless, it's crucial to strike a balance between self-respect and humility. We should not see ourselves as superior to others, but neither should we see ourselves as worthless. We are valuable, not because of our achievements or attributes, but because we are made in God's image.

Self-respect also means taking care of our physical, emotional, and spiritual well-being. It involves making healthy choices, setting boundaries, and avoiding harmful behaviors. After all, as 1 Corinthians 6:19 reminds us, our bodies are temples of the Holy Spirit.

Take a moment to reflect: Do you truly see yourself as fearfully and wonderfully made by God? If not, what steps can you take to cultivate a greater sense of self-respect?

RESPECT FOR OTHERS

Understanding our own worth as God's creation naturally leads us to recognize the same worth in others. As Christians, we are commanded to love our neighbors as ourselves (Mark 12:31), and inherent in that commandment is the call to respect others.

Respect for others means acknowledging their inherent value as individuals made in the image of God. It's about seeing beyond our differences—whether they be of race, culture, social status, or opinion—and recognizing the divine spark in every person.

In the book of Luke, Jesus shares the Golden Rule: *"Do to others as you would have them do to you"* (Luke 6:31). This principle is a call to empathy, urging us to treat others with the same respect and kindness we would wish to receive.

It's worth noting that respect doesn't necessarily mean agreement. We can respect someone as a person and respect their right to hold different beliefs, even if we don't share those beliefs. What's more, we can disagree with someone in a respectful manner, upholding their dignity even as we express our difference in opinion.

RESPECT IN PRACTICE:

TREATING OTHERS AS WE WOULD LIKE TO BE TREATED

The Golden Rule provides a practical guide on how to show respect to others, but what does this look like in everyday life?

Treating others as we would like to be treated involves showing kindness, listening attentively, and speaking courteously. It's about valuing others' opinions, even when they differ from ours. It's about being patient, forgiving, and considerate.

Consider a simple scenario: You're engaged in a heated discussion with a friend. Treating them as you would like to be treated might mean taking a step back, listening to their perspective, and expressing your viewpoint respectfully. It might mean agreeing to disagree, if necessary, but maintaining the friendship despite your differences.

However, the Golden Rule isn't just about how we treat our friends and family; it also applies to how we interact with strangers, those who are different from us, and even those who oppose us. In the Sermon on the Mount, Jesus calls us to love our enemies and pray for those who persecute us (Matthew 5:44). This radical love is an ultimate form of respect, acknowledging the inherent worth of every individual, regardless of their actions.

Let's explore how respect influences our relationships and how we can foster a culture of respect within our families, friendships, and communities. For now, reflect on how you can apply the Golden Rule in your interactions. Are there people in your life whom you need to show more respect? How can you treat them as you would like to be treated?

RESPECT AND RELATIONSHIPS

Respect is the cornerstone of healthy relationships. In families, friendships, and communities, respect fosters understanding, cooperation, and harmony. It promotes mutual growth, enabling each individual to thrive while contributing to the well-being of the group.

In the context of family, respect might look like honoring your parents (Ephesians 6:1-3), listening to your siblings' perspectives, or appreciating your spouse's efforts. Each of these actions acknowledges the value of the other person and their role in your life.

For friendships, respect involves recognizing each other's individuality. It's about supporting each other's goals, appreciating each other's strengths, and accepting each other's weaknesses. Proverbs 27:17 says, *"As iron sharpens iron, so one person sharpens another."* A friendship built on respect can help both individuals grow and become better versions of themselves.

In communities, respect fosters unity and peace. When we respect each other's differences—whether cultural, ideological, or personal—we create an environment where everyone feels valued and accepted. Romans 14:19 advises us to *"make every effort to do what leads to peace and to mutual edification."*

RESPECT FOR AUTHORITY

As Christians, we are also called to respect those in authority. Romans 13:1-2 tells us, *"Let everyone be subject to the governing authorities, for there is no authority except that which God has established... Consequently, whoever rebels against the authority is rebelling against what God has instituted..."*

Respecting authority doesn't mean blindly following orders. Instead, it involves recognizing the role of those in authority, praying for them (1 Timothy 2:1-2), and respectfully voicing our opinions when necessary. It's about balancing obedience to God and respect for human authority.

Ultimately, our final authority is God. When human authorities contradict God's commands, we need to choose to obey God instead. Acts 5:29 guides us: *"We must obey God rather than human beings."* In such cases, we must stand up for what is right while maintaining a respectful attitude.

As we move on to the next section, let's reflect on how respect plays out in our relationships and our attitudes towards authority. Are there areas where we need to show more respect? How can we promote a culture of respect in our families, friendships, and communities?

LIVING WITH RESPECT: A DAILY PRACTICE

Respect is not a one-time act, but a daily practice. It's an attitude that we carry with us, influencing how we interact with the world. Living with respect means embodying the values of empathy, kindness, and humility in our day-to-day lives.

Each day presents countless opportunities to practice respect. When we choose to listen patiently to a friend, help a stranger in need, or acknowledge a colleague's good work, we are practicing respect. Even small acts, like saying "please" and "thank you," are ways of showing respect to others.

Living with respect also means standing up against disrespect when we see it. If we witness someone being treated unfairly, it's our responsibility to speak up, but always in a respectful manner. Proverbs 31:8-9 calls us to *"Speak up for those who cannot speak for themselves, for the rights of all who are destitute. Speak up and judge fairly; defend the rights of the poor and needy."*

Practicing respect can be challenging, especially in difficult situations or with difficult people. Nevertheless, as Christians, we are equipped with the Holy Spirit to guide us and strengthen us during those difficult times.

In this chapter, we have journeyed through the Christian understanding of respect, how it applies to ourselves, to others, and to authority, and how it influences our relationships. We've also looked at how we can incorporate respect into our daily lives.

Respect is a crucial aspect of our Christian walk and is deeply rooted in Christ's teachings. As we strive to live out our faith, let us remember the value of respect and seek to embody it in all our interactions.

CHAPTER 8

STEWARDSHIP

What is stewardship? Whenever we hear this word people think in terms of money, but in reality, the idea of stewardship can apply to all areas of our Christian lives—our environment, bodies, talents, time, the gospel, and all the other resources that God has given us to enjoy. These are all areas that God requires us to be good stewards. In fact, the scripture that comes to mind when God talks about being a good steward is found in the parable of the talents (Matthew 25:14-30). I encourage you to read that parable so that you can better understand God's mind when it comes to the area of stewardship.

UNDERSTANDING STEWARDSHIP

At its core, stewardship is about responsibility. As Christians, we believe that everything we have is a gift from God—our lives, our world, our abilities, even our time. As recipients of these gifts, we're called to care for them responsibly and use them to serve God and others.

The concept of stewardship is introduced early in the Bible, in the book of Genesis. After creating the world and everything in it, God gave humanity a directive: *"Be fruitful and increase in number; fill the earth and subdue it. Rule over the fish in the sea and the birds in the sky and over every living creature that moves on the ground"* (Genesis 1:28). This command, often referred to as the 'Cultural Mandate,' entrusts us with the care and cultivation of the world.

In the New Testament, the apostle Peter emphasizes the idea of stewardship in relation to the gifts we've received from God. He writes, *"Each of you should use whatever gift you have received to serve others, as faithful stewards of God's grace in its various forms"* (1 Peter 4:10). This passage broadens the scope of stewardship beyond physical possessions or the environment, extending it to the talents and abilities we've been given.

STEWARDSHIP OF THE ENVIRONMENT

Stewardship of the environment is a fundamental aspect of our responsibility as Christians. The Bible makes it clear that the earth is the Lord's creation (Psalm 24:1), and we are called to care for it. In Genesis 2:15, we read that *"The Lord God took the man and put him in the Garden of Eden to work it and take care of it."* From the beginning, humans were entrusted with the responsibility to tend and maintain the environment.

So, what does environmental stewardship look like in practice? It involves a range of actions, from small everyday habits to larger lifestyle changes. It could mean reducing waste by recycling or composting, conserving water and energy.

Environmental stewardship also extends to our appreciation and enjoyment of nature. When we take time to marvel at the beauty of a sunset, the complexity of an ecosystem, or the diversity of animal species, we acknowledge the wonder of God's creation. This sense of wonder can inspire us to care for the environment and work towards its preservation.

Let's consider how we can better steward the environment in our daily lives. Are there changes we could make, habits we could adopt, or actions we could take to care for God's creation more effectively? Let's explore this further as we delve into stewardship of our bodies, our talents, and beyond.

STEWARDSHIP OF OUR BODIES

Our bodies are amazing gifts from God, intricately designed and capable of incredible things. As Christians, we believe that our bodies are not only physical vessels but also temples of the Holy Spirit (1 Corinthians 6:19-20). This perspective calls us to be good stewards of our bodies, caring for our physical, mental, and emotional well-being.

One aspect of stewarding our bodies is maintaining good physical health. This can involve eating a balanced diet, exercising regularly, and getting enough sleep. Scripture reminds us of the importance of taking care of our physical health: *"Do you not know that your bodies are temples of the Holy Spirit, who is in you, whom you have received from God? You are not your own; you were bought at a price. Therefore, honor God with your bodies"* (1 Corinthians 6:19-20).

Mental and emotional health is also vital to stewardship of our bodies. This may involve managing stress, seeking support when needed, and engaging in activities that promote relaxation and emotional well-being. The Bible encourages us to guard our hearts and minds, as they influence our thoughts, emotions, and actions: *"Above all else, guard your heart, for everything you do flows from it"* (Proverbs 4:23).

STEWARDSHIP OF OUR TALENTS

Every one of us has unique abilities, talents, and skills—gifts that God has given us to serve Him and others. Stewarding our talents involves recognizing, developing, and using these gifts in ways that bring glory to God and benefit those around us.

The parable of the talents in Matthew 25:14-30 illustrates the importance of using our gifts wisely. In the story, a master entrusts his servants with varying amounts of money (talents) before going on a journey. When he returns, he evaluates how each servant used their talents. The servants who invested and multiplied their talents are commended, while the servant who hid his talent out of fear is rebuked. This parable teaches us that God expects us to use our talents productively and that we'll be held accountable for how we've used them.

To be good stewards of our talents, we need to identify and develop our abilities. This may involve prayer and self-reflection, seeking input from others, or exploring different opportunities to serve. As we grow in our skills and abilities, we can use them to serve God and others in various ways: at home, at work, in our churches, and in our communities.

STEWARDSHIP OF OUR TIME

Time is a precious resource, and as Christians, we're called to be good stewards of the time we've been given. The Apostle Paul reminds us, *"Be very careful, then, how you live— not as unwise but as wise, making the most of every opportunity, because the days are evil"* (Ephesians 5:15-16). This passage encourages us to be intentional with our time, seeking to use it in ways that honor God and serve others.

Balancing our time can be challenging, as we juggle various commitments and responsibilities. As stewards of our time, we should strive to allocate it wisely, balancing work, rest, service, and personal growth. This may involve setting priorities, establishing routines, and being disciplined in managing our schedules.

Stewardship of our resources is a touchy subject for most Christians. This area of a person's life can be very uncomfortable for many Christians to discuss, because it really exposes where our heart lies. Therefore, it is important to be faithful in this area. We need to remember God blesses us with finances to provide for ourselves and others. When we are faithful in this area, we will see the blessings that come from embracing a generous heart as well.

STEWARDSHIP OF OUR RESOURCES

In addition to our time, talents, and bodies, we are also entrusted with various resources—our possessions, finances, and even our relationships. As stewards, we are tasked with managing these resources wisely, responsibly, and with a heart for serving God and others.

Financial stewardship involves managing our money in ways that align with biblical principles. This may include budgeting, saving, avoiding debt, and being generous with our resources. The Bible offers much wisdom on financial stewardship. Proverbs 3:9-10, for example, encourages us to honor God with our wealth, and 2 Corinthians 9:7 underscores the importance of cheerful giving.

Stewardship also extends to our relationships. We are called to nurture and invest in our relationships, showing love, kindness, and respect to others. This reflects the second greatest commandment: *"Love your neighbor as yourself"* (Matthew 22:39).

THE BLESSINGS OF STEWARDSHIP

As we embrace stewardship in all areas of our lives, we experience various blessings. Stewardship cultivates gratitude as we recognize everything we have as a gift from God. It promotes contentment, as we learn to manage and appreciate what we have instead of constantly longing for more.

Stewardship also brings joy as we use our resources, talents, and time to serve others and make a positive impact. As we steward our resources, we experience the joy of giving, the fulfillment of serving, and the peace that comes from living in alignment with God's principles.

Stewardship is a key aspect of our Christian walk. It calls us to be responsible caretakers of the gifts God has given us—our environment, bodies, talents, time, and resources. As we steward these gifts, we honor God, serve others, and experience numerous blessings.

We hope that this exploration of stewardship has been enlightening and encouraging rather than judgmental and condemning. You see, stewardship isn't just about what we have; it's about who has us. As followers of Christ we are called to give in the like manner that God gave and gives. May we continue to grow as faithful stewards, using all that God has given us for His glory and the good of those around us.

CHAPTER 9

GRATITUDE

Gratitude is a fundamental virtue that should be cultivated as we grow in Christ. We, as believers, ought to show gratitude towards God and others. We show gratitude towards God when we obey Him, and thank Him for the work that He wrought for us in Christ. Truthfully, He didn't have to send His Son to die for us. He could have left us to ourselves, but the fact is He loved us enough and proved it by Jesus' death on the cross, and His glorious resurrection. Gratitude is demonstrated through an attitude of thankfulness, so, in light of our recognition of God's blessings, we need to express gratitude in our daily life.

Gratitude, as we will learn, is not just about saying "thank you" but is a way of life that brings us closer to God and opens the door to all the goodness He has in store for us.

UNDERSTANDING GRATITUDE

Exactly what is gratitude? In its simplest form, gratitude is the quality of being thankful; it is a readiness to show appreciation for kindness and to return kindness. From a Christian perspective, gratitude takes on an even deeper meaning. It is an acknowledgment of God's enduring love and mercy towards us. It's a recognition of His grace, even when we don't necessarily feel like we deserve it.

Gratitude is a theme that is woven throughout the Bible. In 1 Thessalonians 5:18, we are reminded to *"give thanks in all circumstances; for this is God's will for you in Christ Jesus."* Similarly, Psalm 107:1 encourages us to *"Give thanks to the LORD, for he is good; his love endures forever."* These verses are just a few of the many that call us to an attitude of thankfulness.

GOD'S BLESSINGS

Recognizing God's blessings in our lives is an essential part of cultivating gratitude. God blesses us in countless ways, both big and small. These blessings might be as monumental as the gift of life itself, or as seemingly small yet essential as our daily bread.

In James 1:17, we are told, *"Every good and perfect gift is from above, coming down from the Father of the heavenly lights, who does not change like shifting shadows."* This verse reassures us that every good thing we experience is a blessing from God. Furthermore, Psalm 103:2 advises us, *"Praise the LORD, my soul, and forget not all his benefits."*

Remembering and recognizing these blessings is a vital step in fostering gratitude. When we take the time to reflect on God's goodness, we are more likely to live with an attitude of thankfulness. But how do we cultivate this attitude and express our gratitude, especially during trials? The following sections of this chapter will delve into these topics more deeply.

CULTIVATING AN ATTITUDE OF THANKFULNESS

Cultivating an attitude of thankfulness is not about ignoring life's difficulties or pretending everything is perfect. Rather, it's about choosing to focus on God's blessings and letting them overshadow our challenges. This may not always be easy, but it's a choice we can make each day, regardless of our circumstances.

Prayer, reflection, and mindfulness are essential tools in cultivating gratitude. By praying, we communicate directly with God, thanking Him for His blessings and asking for the strength to face our challenges. Reflection allows us to look back on our experiences and recognize God's hand in our lives. Mindfulness, or the practice of being fully present in the moment, helps us appreciate the blessings we often overlook in our busy lives.

Several scriptures guide us in this practice. Colossians 3:15-17 says, *"And let the peace of Christ rule in your hearts, to which indeed you were called in one body. And be thankful. Let the word of Christ dwell in you richly, teaching and admonishing one another in all wisdom, singing psalms and hymns and spiritual songs, with thankfulness in your hearts to God. And whatever you do, in word or deed, do everything in the name of the Lord Jesus, giving thanks to God the Father through him."*

Ephesians 5:20 further instructs us to be *"always giving thanks to God the Father for everything, in the name of our Lord Jesus Christ."*

GRATITUDE IN TRIALS

Expressing gratitude amidst hardship might seem counterintuitive. Yet, this is exactly what the Bible encourages us to do. In fact, it's during our most challenging times that gratitude can have the most profound impact on our lives.

Job, despite losing everything he had, managed to express gratitude to God. He said, *"Naked I came from my mother's womb, and naked I will depart. The LORD gave and the LORD has taken away; may the name of the LORD be praised"* (Job 1:21).

Similarly, Paul and Silas, while imprisoned, sang hymns to God, demonstrating their gratitude and faith despite their dire circumstances (Acts 16:25). This serves to show that, even during hard times, God gives us the strength to see things from His perspective, resulting in a gratuitous praise and thankfulness to Him.

Romans 5:3-5 tells us, *"Not only so, but we also glory in our sufferings, because we know that suffering produces perseverance; perseverance, character; and character, hope. And hope does not put us to shame, because God's love has been poured out into our hearts through the Holy Spirit, who has been given to us."* This scripture reminds us that even in our trials, there are reasons to be grateful, as our hardships are often shaping us for better things to come.

EXPRESSING GRATITUDE

Expressing gratitude goes beyond our personal relationship with God. It extends to the people around us as well. A pastor of mine tells those he meets that in order to please God you have to love God and love His people. When we express gratitude, we are acknowledging the good in others, fostering positivity, and encouraging a cycle of kindness.

1 Thessalonians 1:2 reminds us of the importance of expressing gratitude to others: *"We always thank God for all*

of you and continually mention you in our prayers." This is a beautiful example of how we can express gratitude not only to God but also to the people He has placed in our lives.

In the next sections, we will explore the impact of gratitude and provide practical ways to cultivate it in our everyday lives. Stay tuned as we delve deeper into the transformative power of a thankful heart.

THE IMPACT OF GRATITUDE

Gratitude does more than simply make us feel good. It has a transformative effect on our lives and the lives of those around us. Being thankful can improve our physical and mental health, deepen our relationships, and draw us closer to God.

Gratitude fosters contentment by shifting our focus from what we lack to the abundance that we have. This shift in perspective can reduce stress and improve our overall well-being.

Proverbs 17:22 tells us, *"A cheerful heart is good medicine, but a crushed spirit dries up the bones."* A thankful heart is a cheerful heart, and as this scripture suggests, it can have a significant impact on our overall health and well-being.

Furthermore, gratitude can deepen our relationship with God. When we acknowledge our blessings and express our thanks, we recognize our dependence on God. This recognition can lead to a deeper understanding of God's love for us and can strengthen our faith in His providence.

PRACTICAL WAYS TO CULTIVATE GRATITUDE

Cultivating gratitude is a practice that we can incorporate into our daily lives. Here are a few practical ways to do so:

Keep a gratitude journal: Write down three things you are grateful for each day. They can be as simple as a beautiful sunrise, a kind word from a friend, or the food on your table.

Pray regularly: Make it a habit to express your thankfulness to God in your prayers. Thank Him for His love, grace, and the blessings in your life.

Express your appreciation to others: Don't hesitate to tell others when you appreciate them. A simple thank you can go a long way in showing your gratitude and encouraging others.

Serve: Serving others is a practical way to express our gratitude to God. By giving of our time and resources, we acknowledge the blessings we've received and pass them on to others.

Colossians 3:17 reminds us, *"And whatever you do, whether in word or deed, do it all in the name of the Lord Jesus, giving thanks to God the Father through him."*

Gratitude is more than an attitude; it's a lifestyle. As Christians, we are called to live with a spirit of thankfulness, recognizing our countless blessings and expressing our gratitude to God and to those around us.

Thank you, Lord, for Your blessings that you give each and everyone of us. May we be blessed with a thankful heart that overflows with Your love and goodness in Jesus' name Amen.

Chapter 10

Patience & Perseverance

As we journey through life, we will invariably face trials and tribulations, delays and disappointments, and it's during these times that our faith is tested the most. It's also during these times that patience and perseverance become the least desirable and the least to be considered qualities when facing hard times. These two character traits are not just there when we need them but rather they are qualities that are cultivated and developed throughout our lifetime. They are qualities given and cultivated within us by God through life's circumstances in order to conform us into the image of Christ.

Understanding Patience and Perseverance

Before we delve deeper, let's define what we mean by patience and perseverance from a Christian perspective.

Patience, often referred to as long-suffering in the Bible, is the ability to endure difficult circumstances, such as provocation or delay, without becoming annoyed or upset. It's the capacity to remain steadfast and calm, even when faced with adversity. As Colossians 3:12 tells us, *"Therefore, as God's chosen people, holy and dearly loved, clothe yourselves with compassion, kindness, humility, gentleness and patience."*

Perseverance, on the other hand, refers to the quality of continuing steadfastly, especially in something that's difficult or tedious. It's about remaining committed to our faith and our path, even when it's challenging. Romans 5:3-4 extols the virtue of perseverance, stating, *"Not only so, but we also glory in our sufferings, because we know that suffering produces perseverance; perseverance, character; and character, hope."* God works in us and through us with His instrument called suffering. He wields His character within us so that we become more Christlike. You might not be able to say it at the time, but one day you can declare, "Hallelujah! Thank you Lord for the things I have gone through to be able to look more like Your Son."

THE ROLE OF PATIENCE AND PERSEVERANCE IN THE CHRISTIAN LIFE

As followers of Christ, patience and perseverance are indispensable. Our walk with Christ is not always an easy one. We face trials, tests of faith, personal challenges, and even persecution. It's during these times that patience and perseverance come into play.

In Hebrews 12:1, we're told, *"Therefore, since we are surrounded by such a great cloud of witnesses, let us throw off everything that hinders and the sin that so easily entangles. And let us run with perseverance the race marked out for us."* This verse highlights the importance of perseverance in our spiritual journey.

In Galatians 6:9, we read, *"Let us not become weary in doing good, for at the proper time we will reap a harvest if we do not give up."* Here, we see the significance of patience. It encourages us to continue doing good, even when we don't immediately see the fruits of our labor.

These virtues are not just for the difficult times, though. Patience helps us to love others more fully, to bite our tongue when we'd rather lash out, to listen when we'd rather speak. Perseverance helps us to continue growing in our faith, to keep seeking God, even when we don't feel His presence.

In the midst of trials and suffering, there are many factors to consider such as acknowledging God's timing, learning to persevere through difficulties, practicing patience with ourselves and others, and trusting God in the face of delays and disappointments. Although this can result in expressions of depression, loneliness, anxiety, or even fear, we must take heart, and keep trusting that God is working all things together for our good. His good doesn't always match the definition of our good, but rest assured, when our trial is over, it will be good in God's eyes. Remember, during these times God's will is loving, perfect, and holy. He will never leave us nor forsake us (Deuteronomy 31:8: Joshua 1:9;Hebrews 13:5; Mathew 28:20).

GOD'S TIMING AND PATIENCE

One of the most challenging aspects of our walk with God can be understanding and accepting His timing. We often have our own timelines, and our own expectations of when and how things should happen. However, God's timing may not align with ours, and this is where patience becomes crucial.

Ecclesiastes 3:1 reminds us, *"There is a time for everything, and a season for every activity under the heavens."* This scripture underlines the truth that God has a perfect timing for everything in our lives. We may not always understand or agree with it, but we're called to trust in it nonetheless.

Similarly, Habakkuk 2:3 says, *"For the revelation awaits an appointed time; it speaks of the end and will not prove false. Though it linger, wait for it; it will certainly come and will not delay."* Here, we're reassured that even when God's promises seem to be delayed, they will surely come to pass in His perfect timing.

Learning to trust in God's timing requires patience. It may not be easy, and it may stretch our faith, but it's a vital part of our Christian journey.

PERSEVERANCE THROUGH DIFFICULTIES

While patience is about endurance and calmness during delays and provocations, perseverance is about persisting in doing something despite the difficulty or delay in achieving success. The Christian life, while full of joy and peace, is also full of trials and tribulations. It's during these times that perseverance becomes essential.

James 1:12 tells us, *"Blessed is the one who perseveres under trial because, having stood the test, that person will receive the crown of life that the Lord has promised to those who love him."* This scripture affirms the importance of perseverance during trials and the reward that comes with it.

Consider the story of Job in the Bible: despite unimaginable loss and suffering, Job remained faithful to God. His perseverance serves as an example for us all. His story concludes with God restoring his fortunes and giving him twice as much as he had before (Job 42:10).

PATIENCE WITH SELF AND OTHERS

Patience is not just about waiting for God's timing; it's also about our interactions with ourselves and others. We're called to be patient in our personal growth and in our relationships.

Ephesians 4:2 advises, *"Be completely humble and gentle; be patient, bearing with one another in love."* This scripture emphasizes the importance of being patient with others, even when they annoy or provoke us.

Similarly, Colossians 3:12 encourages us, *"Therefore, as God's chosen people, holy and dearly loved, clothe yourselves with compassion, kindness, humility, gentleness and patience."* Here, patience is presented as a virtue that we should clothe ourselves in, a fundamental part of our character as Christians.

In the following sections, we'll delve into how to maintain faith and patience during disappointments and delays, and explore practical ways to develop patience and perseverance.

PATIENCE DURING DISAPPOINTMENTS AND DELAYS

Life can often bring disappointments and delays. Plans don't work out the way we hope, dreams get delayed, and situations don't change as quickly as we'd like. During these times, it can be challenging to remain patient and keep trusting in God's plan.

The Bible offers comforting words during such times. Psalm 27:14 says, *"Wait for the LORD; be strong and take heart and wait for the LORD."* This verse encourages us to stay strong and patient during disappointments, reminding us that our strength comes from the Lord.

Jesus also addressed this in John 16:33, saying, *"In this world you will have trouble. But take heart! I have overcome the world."* Here, Jesus acknowledges the inevitability of troubles in this world, but He also provides reassurance of His victory over these troubles.

CULTIVATING PATIENCE AND PERSEVERANCE

Patience and perseverance are not traits we naturally possess in abundance; they're virtues that need to be cultivated over time. But how do we do this?

Galatians 5:22-23 tells us that patience is a fruit of the Spirit. This means that as we nurture our relationship with God, as we spend time in His Word, in prayer, and in fellowship with other believers, the Holy Spirit works in us to develop this fruit.

Romans 5:3-5 gives us further insight: *"Not only so, but we also glory in our sufferings, because we know that suffering produces perseverance; perseverance, character; and character, hope. And hope does not put us to shame, because God's love has been poured out into our hearts through the Holy Spirit, who has been given to us."* This passage shows us that even our sufferings and trials can be instrumental in developing perseverance.

Patience and perseverance are not optional extras in the Christian life; they're essential traits that we need to cultivate. They enable us to navigate the disappointments, delays, and difficulties of life with grace and hope.

Remember that patience and perseverance are cultivated throughout your journey of faith. They require a daily commitment to trust in God's timing, to remain steadfast during trials, and to be patient with ourselves and others

CHAPTER 11

COMMUNITY AND FELLOWSHIP

Community and fellowship are integral aspects of the Christian life. From the earliest days of the Christian faith, believers have gathered together for worship, learning, encouragement, and service. In this chapter, we'll explore the importance of Christian community, the benefits it brings, and the role of fellowship in our spiritual journeys. Let's delve into practical ways to cultivate strong relationships within the church.

THE IMPORTANCE OF CHRISTIAN COMMUNITY

In the Christian context, a community is more than just a group of people living in the same place or sharing common interests. It's a group of believers who live out their faith together, encouraging one another, bearing each other's burdens, and spurring one another on in love and good deeds.

This idea of community is deeply rooted in the Bible. The book of Acts, for instance, gives us a beautiful picture of the early Christian community. In Acts 2:42-47, we see the believers devoting themselves to the apostles' teaching, fellowship, breaking of bread, and prayer. They shared their possessions, met together daily, and praised God together. This passage highlights the essence of Christian community—mutual love, shared faith, and collective worship.

Community is also important because it reflects the very nature of God. As believers, we understand God as a Trinity— Father, Son, and Holy Spirit—existing in a perfect relationship. In creating us for community, God is inviting us to mirror this divine relationship in our interactions with one another.

THE BENEFITS OF CHRISTIAN COMMUNITY

Being part of a Christian community brings numerous benefits. One of the most significant is spiritual growth. In a Christian community, we are exposed to the wisdom and experiences of other believers. We learn from their insights, get challenged by their questions, and are held accountable for our actions. Proverbs 27:17 puts it this way: *"As iron sharpens iron, so one person sharpens another."*

Christian community also provides support and encouragement in times of need. When we go through trials, our church family is there to comfort us, pray for us, and help meet our needs. This is beautifully illustrated in Ecclesiastes 4:9-12, which tells us that two are better than one because they can help each other in times of need.

Lastly, Christian communities provide opportunities for us to discover and use our spiritual gifts. The apostle Paul talks about this in 1 Corinthians 12:4-7. He explains that we each have different gifts given to us by the Holy Spirit, and these gifts are meant to be used for the common good. In a community, we can use our gifts to serve others and, in turn, be served by their gifts. These gifts are meant to be lived out within the church, and within the world.

Fellowship is very important for growth within the Christian life. That is why we need to cultivate strong relationships within the church. The Christian faith was not meant to be lived out alone but rather it was meant to be lived out in community (Acts 2:37-40).

THE ROLE OF FELLOWSHIP IN CHRISTIAN LIFE

Fellowship, in the Christian context, is more than just spending time together. It is about sharing life, experiences, spiritual insights, and our love for God. It is the communion of believers united by a common faith, purpose, and love for Jesus Christ. The early church fellowship was centered around the apostles doctrine, prayer, and the ordinance of the Lord's supper.

One key scripture that lays out the essence of Christian fellowship is 1 John 1:7, *"But if we walk in the light, as he is in the light, we have fellowship with one another, and the blood of Jesus, his Son, purifies us from all sin."* This verse tells us that when we live in the truth of God's Word and in a right relationship with Him, we naturally have fellowship with each other.

Another significant aspect of fellowship is seen in the early Christian community, as described in Acts 2:42, *"They devoted themselves to the apostles' teaching and to fellowship, to the breaking of bread and to prayer."* This highlights that fellowship was not just about social gatherings but was centered around spiritual activities—learning the Word of God, sharing meals in remembrance of Jesus, and praying together.

CULTIVATING STRONG RELATIONSHIPS WITHIN THE CHURCH

Building strong and meaningful relationships within the church is essential to a vibrant Christian community. These relationships are built on the foundation of love, honesty, and mutual respect. The Apostle Paul, in Romans 12:10, encourages us to, *"Be devoted to one another in love. Honor one another above yourselves."*

However, cultivating these relationships requires intentional effort. It involves regular participation in church activities and being part of smaller groups within the church. These smaller groups often provide a more personal setting where deeper connections can be formed.

Another way to foster strong relationships is through service. Serving together not only enables us to use our God-given gifts but also strengthens our bonds with each other. As we work together for a common purpose, we learn to appreciate each other's strengths and support each other's weaknesses.

Whenever there are people gathered together, problems will occur naturally. This can be in the form of disagreement, hurt, disappointment, but no matter what the problem, we need to learn how to overcome challenges in community and fellowship. There is a role that each individual believer has in the global Church. Each has a gift to use to edify others in His body.

OVERCOMING CHALLENGES IN COMMUNITY AND FELLOWSHIP

Building and maintaining a healthy Christian community is not always easy. Challenges can arise due to differences in personality, viewpoints, or misunderstandings. However, the Bible provides guidance on how to navigate these challenges.

One of the most important biblical instructions for resolving conflicts is found in Matthew 18:15-17. This passage encourages us to approach the person with whom we have a disagreement, privately, first, then with one or two others if the issue isn't resolved, and finally to bring it to the church community if needed. This process promotes a spirit of reconciliation and peace. This ought to be done with gentleness and compassion, with the desired outcome to be repentance and forgiveness.

Another common challenge in community life is dealing with hurt or offense. In such cases, the principle of forgiveness comes into play. Ephesians 4:32 instructs us, *"Be kind and compassionate to one another, forgiving each other, just as in Christ God forgave you."* By choosing to forgive, we reflect God's grace and maintain unity in our community.

THE ROLE OF INDIVIDUAL BELIEVERS IN THE GLOBAL CHURCH

While the focus so far has been on the local church community, it is important to remember that as Christians, we are part of a global Church. This larger community consists of all believers across the world, across various cultures, and across denominations.

As individual believers, we have a role to play in this global Church. We are called to pray for the worldwide

Church, especially for those who are persecuted for their faith. We can also contribute by supporting mission work, either through financial contributions or by volunteering our time and skills.

The Apostle Paul writes in 1 Corinthians 12:26, *"If one part suffers, every part suffers with it; if one part is honored, every part rejoices with it."* This verse reminds us of our interconnectedness as the body of Christ, urging us to empathize with and support our fellow believers within the local church and around the world.

Community and fellowship are vital aspects of the Christian life. They provide a space for us to grow spiritually, support one another, and serve collectively. Despite the challenges that might arise, the Bible offers guidance on how to foster a loving, forgiving, and supportive community. We need to remember Jesus shed His blood and died and placed us in a body where we can proclaim His name to the world. The church has been established and ordained by God; therefore, we need not to forsake assembling ourselves together (Hebrews 10:25-26).

As we wrap up this chapter, We hope you feel encouraged to actively participate in your Christian community and cherish the fellowship you share with other believers. Support those in your local body through prayer, encouragement, generosity, which all require expression in community with other like minded individuals.

CHAPTER 12

HUMILITY

Humility, from a Christian perspective, is not about thinking less of yourself; it's about thinking of yourself less and of others and God more. It involves recognizing our dependence on God and respecting the worth and value of others. In this chapter, we will explore the concept of humility, see it in action in the life of Jesus, and discuss how we can cultivate it in our daily lives.

UNDERSTANDING HUMILITY

When we talk about humility, what do we mean? The word humility comes from the Latin root 'humus,' meaning 'ground.' Humility, then, is about being 'grounded' or 'down to earth.' It involves having a realistic view of ourselves, acknowledging both our strengths and limitations.

Contrary to some misconceptions, humility is not about having low self-esteem or being self-deprecating. It's not about seeing ourselves as worthless or always putting ourselves down. Instead, it is about seeing ourselves accurately, neither as better nor worse than we truly are. We are to see ourselves and others from God's perspective. When we do this we will know how to live before God with the right mindset.

The Bible offers great wisdom on humility. For instance, Proverbs 22:4 says, *"Humility is the fear of the Lord; its wages are riches and honor and life."* This verse points to the recognition of our place in relation to God, acknowledging Him as God and ourselves as His creation.

HUMILITY IN THE LIFE OF JESUS

If we're looking for a model of perfect humility, we need look no further than Jesus. Throughout His earthly ministry, Jesus consistently demonstrated humility in His interactions with others and in His relationship with God the Father.

One powerful example of Jesus' humility is found in John 13, where Jesus washes His disciples' feet. In the culture of the time, foot washing was a task reserved for the lowest servants. Yet, Jesus, the Master and Teacher, willingly took on this role. He told His disciples, *"I have set you an example that you should do as I have done for you"* (John 13:15).

Jesus' humility was also vividly demonstrated in His crucifixion. Though He was innocent, Jesus willingly endured shame, suffering, and death on a cross. He did this out of obedience to God the Father and out of love for us. As Philippians 2:8 says, *"And being found in appearance as a man, he humbled himself by becoming obedient to death—even death on a cross!"*

These instances from Jesus' life give us a clear picture of what true humility looks like. It involves putting others' needs above our own, being willing to serve, and surrendering our will to God's. As we continue through this chapter, we'll explore more about how to cultivate this kind of humility in our own lives.

THE IMPORTANCE OF HUMILITY IN CHRISTIAN LIFE

Humility holds a significant place in Christian life, not only because it was exemplified by Jesus, but also because it shapes how we interact with God and others. Humility is the soil in which other virtues grow; it allows us to be teachable, patient, forgiving, and compassionate.

1 Peter 5:5-6 says, *"All of you, clothe yourselves with humility toward one another, because, 'God opposes the proud but shows favor to the humble.' Humble yourselves, therefore, under God's mighty hand, that he may lift you up in due time."* Here, the Bible clearly links humility with receiving God's favor and grace.

Humility allows us to recognize our need for God's grace. It prompts us to rely on Him instead of trying to live in our own strength. In acknowledging our limitations, we make room for God's power to work in and through us (2 Corinthians 12:9).

PRACTICAL WAYS TO CULTIVATE HUMILITY

While humility is a divine virtue, it doesn't magically appear in our lives. It's something we need to consciously cultivate and practice. Here are some practical ways to do that:

Self-Reflection: Regularly take time to reflect on your actions, thoughts, and motivations. Consider whether they align with humility or are driven by pride or self-centeredness.

Service: Look for opportunities to serve others, particularly in ways that may not be recognized or rewarded.

Gratitude: Cultivate an attitude of gratitude. Recognizing the gifts you've received can help you remember your dependence on God and others.

Empathy: Practice seeing things from others' perspectives. This can help you appreciate their experiences and value their contributions.

Prayer: Include humility in your prayers. Ask God to cultivate this virtue in you and to reveal areas where you need to grow.

Remember, humility isn't about devaluing yourself. It's about accurately understanding your value in relation to God and others. It's about recognizing that we all are God's beloved creations, equally in need of His grace.

THE CHALLENGE OF HUMILITY

As we seek to cultivate humility, we should be aware that it's not always easy. It can be especially challenging in a culture that often values self-promotion and 'looking out for number one.' Yet, the rewards of humility are profound. As Proverbs 11:2 reminds us, *"When pride comes, then comes disgrace, but with humility comes wisdom."*

We'll continue our journey into the virtues that make up a Christian life in the next chapter. For now, let's keep in mind the humble example of Jesus and seek to follow in His footsteps.

Humility in Relationships

Humility is a powerful virtue that impacts all our relationships. With humility, we can more easily forgive, be patient, show respect, and express genuine love. We can better empathize with others and be a source of comfort and understanding.

Consider Philippians 2:3-4, which says, *"Do nothing out of selfish ambition or vain conceit. Rather, in humility value others above yourselves, not looking to your own interests but each of you to the interests of the others."* This scripture beautifully illustrates how humility can transform our relationships, leading us to value others and their interests.

Humility and Leadership

Even in positions of authority or leadership, humility plays a vital role. Christian leaders are called to serve, not to be served, following the example of Jesus, who washed the feet of His disciples in an act of humble service (John 13:12-17). A humble leader listens, learns, and leads with love, recognizing that leadership is about service rather than power.

Overcoming the Obstacles to Humility

In our journey to cultivate humility, we may encounter obstacles such as pride, fear of being overlooked, or the desire for recognition and praise. However, we can overcome these challenges by constantly reminding ourselves of Jesus' example and God's word. Scriptures such as James 4:10, which says, *"Humble yourselves before the Lord, and He will lift you up,"* can offer comfort and guidance.

THE JOY OF HUMILITY

Cultivating humility brings joy and peace into our lives. It helps us appreciate God's grace, promotes harmonious relationships, and aligns us more closely with Jesus' teachings. As we conclude this chapter, may we strive to live out the words of Micah 6:8: *"He has shown you, O mortal, what is good. And what does the LORD require of you? To act justly and to love mercy and to walk humbly with your God."*

CHAPTER 13

HOPE & JOY

Two of the most beautiful aspects of the Christian life are hope and joy. These twin virtues have their roots in God's love and promises, and, as such, they can illuminate even the darkest corners of our lives. Let's look at what hope and joy mean from a Christian perspective, their importance in our spiritual walk, and how they can persist even in times of hardship. As we delve into these topics, we'll discover together that hope and joy are not just feelings but choices that can deeply influence our lives and the lives of those around us.

UNDERSTANDING HOPE

When we speak of hope in a Christian context, we're not talking about a vague wish or a simple optimism. Christian hope is a confident expectation, a firm assurance about things that are unseen and still in the future. It's not about wishful thinking, but a certain anticipation of God's promises and His trustworthiness.

Consider Hebrews 11:1, *"Now faith is confidence in what we hope for and assurance about what we do not see."* Here, we see hope intimately linked with faith—faith is the confidence in our hope. This is the hope we're called to—a hope that stands firm even when the storms of life blow.

UNDERSTANDING JOY

Joy, on the other hand, is a deep and powerful emotion that springs from the soul. It is more than mere happiness, which is often dependent on our circumstances. Joy is a fruit of the Spirit (Galatians 5:22), a gift that permeates our lives regardless of what's happening around us.

In Nehemiah 8:10, we find these words: *"The joy of the LORD is your strength."* This verse beautifully captures the essence of Christian joy—it's not based on our abilities, our circumstances, or our efforts, but on God's unchanging nature. Even in the middle of trials and tribulations, this joy gives us strength, reminding us that God is in control and He is working all things for our good.

The intertwining of hope and joy provides a solid foundation for us as we navigate through life. As we grow in understanding these virtues, we'll see that they are not just abstract concepts, but tangible realities that can shape our daily living. In the next sections, we'll delve into the source of our hope and joy, and discover how we can hold onto them, even in the midst of life's storms.

THE SOURCE OF OUR HOPE AND JOY

Our hope and joy are deeply rooted in God and His promises. In Romans 15:13, Paul prays, *"May the God of hope fill you with all joy and peace as you trust in him, so that you may* overflow with hope by the power of the Holy Spirit." This verse encapsulates the source of our hope and joy—God Himself. We don't conjure these up; they are gifts from our Heavenly Father, springing from our trust in Him and empowered by the Holy Spirit.

Jesus, too, speaks of this in John 15:11 when He says, "*I have told you this so that my joy may be in you and that your joy may be complete.*" Jesus doesn't merely give us joy, He offers His joy—the joy that sustained Him through the cross and the grave. This divine joy, rooted in God's love and promises, is what makes our joy complete. And it's this joy that allows us to rejoice even in the face of difficulties.

HOPE AND JOY IN DIFFICULT TIMES

In a world filled with pain, loss, and uncertainty, how do we hold on to our hope and joy? The first Christians provide us with an inspiring example. In Acts 5:41, we read about the apostles rejoicing after being flogged because they had been considered worthy of suffering disgrace for the Name of Jesus. They had a hope that wasn't dimmed by their circumstances, and a joy that couldn't be quenched by suffering.

Romans 5:3-5 also provides insight: "*Not only so, but we also glory in our sufferings, because we know that suffering produces perseverance; perseverance, character; and character, hope. And hope does not put us to shame, because God's love has been poured out into our hearts through the Holy Spirit, who has been given to us.*" Suffering, instead of destroying our hope and joy, can refine them and lead us to a deeper experience of God's love.

CULTIVATING HOPE AND JOY

Cultivating hope and joy isn't about ignoring the reality of pain or difficulty. It's about choosing to trust God's promises despite our circumstances. It's about clinging to God's character—His love, faithfulness, and goodness—even when we can't see the way forward.

There are practical ways we can cultivate these virtues. Regular prayer and meditation on God's Word can help us keep our focus on God's promises rather than our problems. Fellowship with other believers can provide encouragement and remind us that we're not alone. Serving others can shift our perspective and give us a glimpse of God's kingdom at work. Practicing gratitude can remind us of God's blessings and His faithfulness in the past, fueling our hope and joy for the future.

In the next part of the chapter, we'll explore these practices in more depth, providing practical tips and guidance on how to cultivate hope and joy in your daily life.

PRACTICAL WAYS TO NURTURE HOPE AND JOY

Practical actions are integral to nurturing hope and joy. They are like spiritual exercises that strengthen our inner selves and facilitate growth in these virtues. Here are some practical ways to nurture hope and joy:

Prayer: Philippians 4:6-7 advises us to present our requests to God with thanksgiving, promising that God's peace will guard our hearts and minds in Christ Jesus. Regular, honest prayer can help us maintain a hopeful and joyful perspective, even when circumstances are challenging.

Meditation on God's Word: Scriptures are filled with promises of God's faithfulness, love, and power. By regularly meditating on these promises, we can anchor our hope and joy in God's unchanging character and unfailing promises. Verses like Romans 15:13, Psalm 16:11, and 1 Peter 1:8-9 can be especially encouraging.

Fellowship: Christian fellowship is a vital source of encouragement and support (Hebrews 10:24-25). By sharing our struggles and victories, we can encourage each other to hold onto hope and joy.

Serving Others: Serving others can take our eyes off our problems and help us see God at work in the world. Plus, there's a unique joy that comes from serving others in love (Acts 20:35).

Practicing Gratitude: Practicing gratitude can shift our focus from what's wrong to what's right, fostering a mindset of hope and joy. The Psalms are filled with expressions of gratitude to God and can serve as a model for us.

MAINTAINING HOPE AND JOY

Maintaining hope and joy is a lifelong journey. It requires persistence, patience, and a continual reliance on God. It's not about the absence of pain or hardship but about learning to see God's hand at work even in the midst of them. The apostle Paul exemplifies this beautifully. Despite being imprisoned, he wrote letters filled with hope and joy, such as Philippians, reminding believers to rejoice in the Lord always.

Remember, hope and joy are not based on our circumstances but on God's unchanging character and promises. As you walk with God, let His Word, His Spirit, and His people remind you of the hope and joy that are yours in Christ.

We've explored the Christian virtues of hope and joy. We've seen that they are gifts from God, rooted in His character and promises. We've also looked at how we can nurture these virtues and maintain them, even in challenging times. As we conclude, We encourage you to lean into these practices, asking God to deepen your experience of hope and joy.

CHAPTER 14

BIBLE STUDY

B ible study is vital for our Christian growth and maturity. Just as our bodies need physical food to grow and stay healthy, our spirits need the spiritual food that comes from God's Word. Through Bible study, we have a direct line to God's thoughts, His promises, His commands, and His love for us. Bible study is so important and how you study the Bible is just as important as reading it. When done properly it will have a transformative effect on your life.

WHAT IS BIBLE STUDY?

Bible study is more than just reading the Bible; it's a dedicated, focused exploration of God's Word. It's about taking the time to really dive into the scriptures, to understand the context, the message, and the application for our lives. This is important to understand because Bible study is not about what the scripture means to you as the reader.

The student of the Bible is to seek to understand what the author was saying to the original audience, and in doing so, they are to take the principles given to the original audience and then begin to apply them to their own life. If not done properly there can be false understandings of God, His character, and a false understanding of who we are as Christians.

In Bible study, we're not just skimming the surface, but we're going deep, seeking to understand God's message to us. It's like being a spiritual detective, looking for clues and connections, understanding the context, and discovering the life-changing truths that God has for us.

The Bible itself encourages this kind of deep exploration. In 2 Timothy 2:15 (ESV), Paul writes to Timothy, *"Do your best to present yourself to God as one approved, a worker who has no need to be ashamed, rightly handling the word of truth."* And in Joshua 1:8 (NIV), God commands Joshua, *"Keep this Book of the Law always on your lips; meditate on it day and night, so that you may be careful to do everything written in it. Then you will be prosperous and successful."*

THE IMPORTANCE OF BIBLE STUDY

Why is Bible study so important? First and foremost, Bible study is how we get to know God. The Bible is God's revealed Word to us: it's His way of communicating His character, His promises, His plan for humanity, and His love for each one of us.

Through Bible study, we gain wisdom and guidance for our lives. Psalm 119:105 (NIV) says, *"Your word is a lamp to my feet and a light to my path."* The more we study the Bible, the more light we have to guide our decisions and our actions.

Bible study also helps us grow spiritually. As we understand and apply God's Word in our lives, we become more like Jesus. We're transformed by the renewing of our minds (Romans 12:2), our faith increases (Romans 10:17), and we're equipped for every good work (2 Timothy 3:16-17).

The Holy Spirit helps us in our Bible study, He enables us to understand the Bible, so that is why we should pray and ask God for His help to understand what we're about to read. The most important thing is not to let the challenge of Bible study overwhelm you. This book is meant to help you in this journey.

THE ROLE OF THE HOLY SPIRIT IN BIBLE STUDY

One of the incredible gifts that Jesus left us was the Holy Spirit. Jesus referred to the Holy Spirit as the "Helper" (John 14:16), and when it comes to Bible study, the Holy Spirit indeed plays an instrumental role.

The Holy Spirit helps us understand the scriptures. As we read in 1 Corinthians 2:14 (NIV), *"The person without the Spirit does not accept the things that come from the Spirit of God but considers them foolishness, and cannot understand them because they are discerned only through the Spirit."*

As you approach Bible study, remember to invite the Holy Spirit into your time of reading and reflection. Ask Him to illuminate the scriptures, to give you understanding, and to show you how to apply God's Word in your life. Bible study isn't merely an intellectual exercise; it's a spiritual journey guided by the Holy Spirit.

APPROACHING THE BIBLE

The Bible is a unique book. It's not like a novel that you read from beginning to end. It's a collection of books, letters, poems, prophecies, and historical accounts, each with its own context and message.

When approaching the Bible, it's important to understand its structure. The Bible is divided into two main sections: the Old Testament and the New Testament. The Old Testament, among other things, tells the story of the Israelites and contains the laws given by God to His people. The New Testament tells the story of Jesus, the early Christians, and contains letters written by apostles like Paul, Peter, and John.

It's also important to recognize the different genres within the Bible. There are books of law (like Leviticus), history (like 1 & 2 Kings), poetry (like Psalms), prophecy (like Isaiah), gospels (like Mark), letters/epistles (like Romans), and apocalyptic literature (like Revelation). Each genre has a unique style and should be approached differently.

PRACTICAL TIPS FOR EFFECTIVE BIBLE STUDY

Here are some practical tips to help you study the Bible effectively:

Pray before you start: Before you open your Bible, spend a few moments in prayer. Ask God to open your heart and mind to understand His Word.

Choose a specific book or passage to study: Rather than randomly opening the Bible and reading, choose a specific book or passage for your study. You could decide to study a specific book of the Bible or follow a Bible reading plan.

Read slowly and carefully: Take your time to read each verse. Don't rush through it.

Take notes: Jot down your observations, questions, and thoughts as you read. This will help you process what you're reading and remember it better.

Use a study Bible: A study Bible includes notes and commentary that can help you understand difficult passages and the historical and cultural context.

Meditate on the Word: After reading a passage, spend some time thinking about it. Ask yourself, "What is God saying to me through this scripture?"

In the next sections, we'll discuss how to overcome challenges in Bible study, the role of Bible study in building our faith, and how Bible study impacts our day-to-day living.

Overcoming Challenges in Bible Study

Every Christian will experience difficulties when trying to study the Bible at some point or another. It's perfectly normal, and there are ways to overcome these challenges. Let's look at a few:

Understanding difficult passages: Not every part of the Bible is easy to understand. When you come across a difficult passage, don't skip over it. Instead, take the time to research it. Consult various translations, use Bible commentaries, and don't hesitate to ask others (like a pastor, mentor, or trusted friend) for their insight. Remember, the goal is not just to read the Bible but to understand it.

Consistency: One of the hardest parts of Bible study is being consistent. Life gets busy, and it's easy to push Bible study aside. Try to set a regular time each day for Bible study, even if it's only for a few minutes. Consistency is key to forming a habit.

Distractions: It's easy to get distracted during Bible study. Try to find a quiet place where you can focus. If you find your mind wandering, don't be too hard on yourself. Gently redirect your attention back to the scripture you are studying.

BIBLE STUDY AND FAITH

Studying the Bible is crucial for growing and strengthening our faith. Romans 10:17 (NIV) says, *"Consequently, faith comes from hearing the message, and the message is heard through the word about Christ."* As we immerse ourselves in God's Word, our understanding of His character deepens, and our faith grows.

BIBLE STUDY IN EVERYDAY LIFE

Bible study is not just an intellectual exercise; it's meant to transform our lives. James 1:22 (NIV) instructs us, *"Do not merely listen to the word, and so deceive yourselves. Do what it says."* As we study the Bible, we should always be asking, "How does this apply to my life?" and "How can I live out what I've learned?"

BIBLE STUDY TECHNIQUES

There are various techniques to study the Bible, and everyone might have their preferred methods. Let's explore a few that could be helpful for you:

SOAP Method (Scripture, Observation, Application, Prayer): This is a simple yet powerful method for studying the Bible. Start by selecting a Scripture passage. Make Observations about the text. Apply the text to your life. End with Prayer.

Inductive Bible Study: This method involves three steps: observation (what does the passage say?), interpretation (what does the passage mean?), and application (how should this passage change me?).

Verse Mapping: This technique involves selecting a verse and then studying it in depth. Look at different translations, study the context in which it was written, and explore the original Greek or Hebrew words.

Topical Study: Pick a topic (like faith, love, or patience) and study all the Bible verses and passages related to that topic. This is a great way to get a comprehensive understanding of what the Bible says about specific subjects.

THE ROLE OF THE HOLY SPIRIT IN BIBLE STUDY

The Holy Spirit plays a critical role in Bible study. John 14:26 (NIV) says, *"But the Advocate, the Holy Spirit, whom the Father will send in my name, will teach you all things and will remind you of everything I have said to you."* When studying the Bible, always pray for the Holy Spirit to guide you into all truth and to help you understand and apply God's Word.

THE LIFELONG JOURNEY OF BIBLE STUDY

Bible study is not a task to be completed, but a lifelong journey. The more we study God's Word, the more we'll grow in our love for Him and our understanding of His will for our lives. May you be blessed in your journey of studying God's Word and drawing closer to Him.

CHAPTER 15

WITNESSING & SHARING THE GOSPEL

To be a Christian is to be a witness, and to witness is to share the good news of Jesus Christ. It's a call that echoes through our lives, from the moment we first grasp the depth of God's love for us, to every encounter we have with others. In this chapter, we'll explore what it means to witness, the role of the Holy Spirit in witnessing, and Jesus as our ultimate example of how to share the Gospel.

WHAT IS WITNESSING?

To witness, in the Christian context, is to share your personal experiences of God's grace, to tell the story of Jesus' love, and to explain how faith in Him has transformed your life. It is a testimony of belief and the impact of that belief on your life. To witness is to spread the "Good News" or Gospel of Jesus Christ to those around you.

Let's look at a few verses that illustrate this. In Matthew 28:19-20, Jesus gives what is now known as the Great

Commission: *"Go therefore and make disciples of all nations, baptizing them in the name of the Father and of the Son and of the Holy Spirit, teaching them to observe all that I have commanded you."*

This command from Jesus makes it clear that sharing the Gospel isn't a suggestion or a task meant only for pastors and church leaders. It's a vital responsibility for every person who follows Him.

THE ROLE OF THE HOLY SPIRIT IN WITNESSING

The Holy Spirit plays a crucial role in witnessing. When Jesus ascended to heaven, He sent the Holy Spirit to guide, empower, and equip believers to continue His work on earth, including the work of evangelism.

In Acts 1:8, Jesus tells His disciples, *"But you will receive power when the Holy Spirit has come upon you, and you will be my witnesses in Jerusalem and in all Judea and Samaria, and to the end of the earth."* The Holy Spirit gives us the power to be effective witnesses. He helps us to speak with courage and conviction, He guides us to people who are ready to hear the Gospel, and He works in their hearts to help them understand and accept the truth.

We need to look at Jesus as our example in witnessing, the importance of preparing to witness, and practical ways to share the Gospel.

Remember, witnessing isn't about having all the answers or convincing someone through our own power and logic. It's about sharing the love and grace of God, as shown through Jesus, and trusting the Holy Spirit to do the rest. The Holy Spirit is the one who changes hearts and therefore it is important to pray before sharing, asking God to grant to you the ability to share and give those who listen the ability to receive and respond to the message.

JESUS AS OUR EXAMPLE IN WITNESSING

Jesus is the perfect example of how to share the Gospel. He used various methods to reach different people, showing us that there is no one-size-fits-all approach to witnessing. He often used parables, which are stories with a deeper meaning, to teach about God's Kingdom. He also performed miracles that demonstrated God's power and love.

Perhaps most importantly, Jesus showed us that effective witnessing is about building relationships and meeting people where they are. Whether He was talking to a crowd, a small group, or an individual, Jesus always communicated with empathy and understanding.

An excellent example of this is found in John 4, where Jesus talks with the Samaritan woman at the well. Despite the cultural and religious barriers between them, Jesus engages with her respectfully and compassionately, leading her to recognize him as the Messiah.

PREPARING TO WITNESS

Preparing to witness is an essential part of the process. It involves knowing the Gospel message, understanding the person you're witnessing to, and being ready to answer questions.

1 Peter 3:15 advises us, *"But in your hearts revere Christ as Lord. Always be prepared to give an answer to everyone who asks you to give the reason for the hope that you have. But do this with gentleness and respect."*

In the next section, we'll discuss practical ways to share the Gospel, which will include tips for preparing to witness.

PRACTICAL WAYS TO SHARE THE GOSPEL

Sharing the Gospel isn't about delivering a well-rehearsed speech. It's about having authentic conversations about faith, asking questions, listening carefully, and sharing your experiences with God. Here are a few practical ways to share the Gospel:

Share your personal testimony: Tell others about your experiences with God. How has faith in Jesus changed your life?

Use the Bible: The Bible is our most important tool in sharing the Gospel. Share Bible stories and verses that have been meaningful to you.

Show love and kindness: Sometimes, the most powerful testimony we can give is the way we live our lives. Show God's love through your actions.

Remember, witnessing is an ongoing process. It's not just about one conversation; it's about consistently demonstrating God's love and being ready to share the Gospel when opportunities arise.

In the next section, we'll discuss respectful witnessing and how to share your faith without being disrespectful or intrusive.

RESPECTFUL WITNESSING

Sharing the Gospel is a delicate task that requires sensitivity and respect. We must remember that everyone has their own beliefs and experiences, and it's important to respect these as we share our faith.

Here are some guidelines for respectful witnessing:

Listen more than you speak: Understand where the person is coming from. Ask questions about their beliefs and genuinely listen to their responses. This will show them that you respect their thoughts and opinions.

Don't argue or debate: The purpose of sharing the Gospel is not to win an argument but to communicate God's love. If the conversation becomes heated or argumentative, it's best to steer it back to a more peaceful tone or pause and resume at another time.

Be patient and understanding: Change doesn't happen overnight. People may need time to process what you've shared with them. Don't rush them or pressure them into making a decision.

Practice empathy: Try to understand the other person's perspective. This will help you communicate more effectively and compassionately.

Scripture guides us in this as well, as Colossians 4:6 says, *"Let your conversation be always full of grace, seasoned with salt, so that you may know how to answer everyone."*

OVERCOMING FEAR IN WITNESSING

It's natural to feel nervous or afraid when sharing your faith, especially if you're worried about rejection or misunderstanding. But remember that God is with you, and he will give you the words to say. As Jesus promised in Matthew 28:20, *"And surely I am with you always, to the very end of the age."*

One practical way to overcome fear is to pray before you witness. Ask God to give you courage, wisdom, and the right words to say. Also, practicing with a friend or a family member can also help build your confidence.

Sharing the Gospel is an act of obedience to the great commission (Mark 16:15). We should pray that God would allow us the opportunity to share the love and hope we've in Jesus with others. Remember that effective witnessing is not about your ability or inabilities. The results of witnessing are totally dependent on the sovereign act of God in the hearts of man by the Holy Spirit. You could have all the answers to questions or have the ability to convince someone to believe what you believe, but that does not mean you will see results (Acts 26:28). It's about sharing your faith in a loving, respectful way and trusting God to do what He does best.

CHAPTER 16

LIVING A CHRIST-CENTERED LIFE

Our goal for this book is to integrate everything we've learned in order to help us live a life centered on Christ. This chapter serves as an encouraging call to action and as a beacon guiding you towards a fulfilling, Christ-centered life.

RECAP OF THE JOURNEY

Throughout this book, hopefully, you have discovered, like us, the foundational aspects of our faith. We pray that you've found them not only instructive but inspiring. Let's take a moment to recall our journey:

We started with understanding the role of Faith in our lives, recognizing that *"faith is the assurance of things hoped for, the conviction of things not seen"* (Hebrews 11:1).

Then, we delved into the power of Prayer, reminding ourselves to *"pray without ceasing"* (1 Thessalonians 5:17).

Our exploration of Love & Forgiveness taught us to *"Above all, love each other deeply, because love covers over a multitude of sins"* (1 Peter 4:8).

And so forth, we went through the chapters on Compassion & Service, Integrity, Respect, Stewardship, Gratitude, Patience & Perseverance, Community & Fellowship, Humility, Hope & Joy, Bible Study, and Witnessing & Sharing the Gospel.

Each of these elements is vital, weaving together to form a rich tapestry of the Christian life.

WHAT DOES IT MEAN TO LIVE A CHRIST-CENTERED LIFE?

Living a Christ-centered life means that Christ is at the heart of everything we do. It means inviting Him into every area of our lives, from our personal decisions to our interactions with others. When we say that we live a Christ-centered life, we're saying that we've made Jesus the Lord of our lives. He's not just a part of our lives; He's at the very core and center of every action and decision we seek to make.

The Bible says, *"I have been crucified with Christ. It is no longer I who live, but Christ who lives in me. And the life I now live in the flesh I live by faith in the Son of God, who loved me and gave himself for me"* (Galatians 2:20). This verse beautifully encapsulates what it means to live a Christ-centered life. It's a life lived in faith, fueled by Christ's love for us, and dedicated to His glory.

Furthermore, living a Christ-centered life means seeking to reflect Christ in our actions. As Colossians 3:17 exhorts, *"And whatever you do, in word or deed, do everything in the name of the Lord Jesus, giving thanks to God the Father through him."*

Whether we're at school, at work, with our families, or among friends, our goal should be to honor Jesus in all we do.

What does this look like in everyday life? What is the impact of a Christ-centered life and what are some practical steps to incorporate Christ's teachings into our daily lives?

THE IMPACT OF A CHRIST-CENTERED LIFE

Living a Christ-centered life transforms us from the inside out. It reshapes our thoughts, influences our actions, and colors our interactions with others.

Personal Transformation: When Christ is at the center of our lives, we undergo a personal transformation. We begin to bear the fruit of the Spirit: *"love, joy, peace, patience, kindness, goodness, faithfulness, gentleness, self-control"* (Galatians 5:22-23). These attributes start to define us, improving our character and making us more like Jesus.

Influence on Others: A Christ-centered life also impacts those around us. When we reflect Christ's love and kindness, we become a light to others (Matthew 5:14). Our words and actions can direct people towards Jesus, influencing their perception of Christianity and possibly their eternal destiny.

Eternal Perspective: Living a Christ-centered life provides an eternal perspective. We understand that our time on earth is temporary and that our ultimate home is with God. This perspective gives us a sense of purpose and hope, knowing that our life has eternal significance.

PRACTICAL WAYS TO LIVE A CHRIST-CENTERED LIFE

Here are some practical ways you can live a Christ-centered life:

Prayer and Bible Study: Maintain a regular prayer life and commit to studying God's Word. These spiritual disciplines will help you grow closer to God and understand His will for your life. As Psalm 119:105 says, "Your word is a lamp to my feet and a light to my path."

Community and Fellowship: Surround yourself with fellow believers who can encourage you, pray for you, and walk alongside you in your Christian journey. "And let us consider how to stir up one another to love and good works, not neglecting to meet together, as is the habit of some, but encouraging one another, and all the more as you see the Day drawing near." (Hebrews 10:24-25)

Service: Look for opportunities to serve others, both within your church and in your broader community. Jesus taught us to be servants, and by following His example, we show His love to others.

Sharing the Gospel: Share your faith with others. You can do this through your actions, your words, and your lifestyle. Be ready to give an answer to anyone who asks about the hope you have (1 Peter 3:15).

TRUSTING IN JESUS AS YOUR LORD AND SAVIOR

To truly live a Christ-centered life, you must first trust in Jesus as your Lord and Savior. This means acknowledging your sin, believing that Jesus died for your sins and rose from the dead, for you. It is to believe Jesus' death on the cross was for you. You believe His act of obedience to the Father and bearing the punishment on the cross was taken for you. You believe Jesus took the punishment reserved for you. Then you believe that Him rising from the dead means your justification, and complete forgiveness. This is followed by confession that Jesus is your Lord and Savior. This means you will now submit to Him and follow Him according to what's revealed in the Word of God. Romans 10:9 tells us, *"If you confess with your mouth that Jesus is Lord and believe in your heart that God raised him from the dead, you will be saved."* This is not an intellectual exercise but it is a Spiritual birth because the Holy Spirit enables you to believe and confess that Jesus is Lord (1 Corinthians 12:3; Romans 8:15; Galatians 4:6).

If you haven't yet made this decision to trust in Christ and would like to, we invite you to pray a prayer of commitment. Remember, there's no special formula for this prayer. It's simply a conversation with God where you acknowledge the depth of your sinfulness and your need for Him, confess your sins, and trust in Jesus as your Lord and Savior. This means abandoning any idea of merit based on what you have accomplished, not trusting in religious affiliation, upbringing, or any other act or thought. Only in Christ do you have forgiveness and salvation, and it is based on what He has done and not what you have done or will do.

NAVIGATING CHALLENGES AND DOUBTS

It's important to understand that living a Christ-centered life doesn't mean you won't face challenges or doubts. In fact, Jesus told us that in this world we will have trouble, but we can take heart because He has overcome the world (John 16:33).

Facing Challenges: When challenges arise, remember to lean on God. Seek His guidance through prayer and Bible study. Rely on the strength and peace that only He can provide. Remember the words of Philippians 4:13, *"I can do all things through Christ who strengthens me."*

Dealing with Doubts: If you experience doubts, don't be discouraged. Doubts can be an opportunity for growth if they lead you to seek answers and deepen your understanding of God. Don't hesitate to ask questions and seek guidance from trusted spiritual mentors.

THE JOURNEY AHEAD

Living a Christ-centered life is a journey. It's not about being perfect, but about continually growing and striving to be more like Jesus each day.

Continual Growth: Always seek to grow in your relationship with God. Keep learning, praying, and striving to apply God's Word to your life.

Spiritual Milestones: Celebrate spiritual milestones and remember God's faithfulness. Reflect on how far you've come in your spiritual journey and anticipate where God is leading you next.

Living a Christ-centered life is the most rewarding and fulfilling life you can lead. It provides purpose, peace, and an eternal perspective that surpasses all worldly pursuits. As you embark on this journey, remember the words of Proverbs 3:5-6, *"Trust in the Lord with all your heart and lean not on your own understanding; in all your ways submit to him, and he will make your paths straight."*

Remember, you're not on this journey alone. We want to encourage you to be a part of a community of believers, so that you can learn and grow from others pursuing Christ as you are. Of equal importance is to pray that God reveals your spiritual gifts so that you can serve in the church. Remember, you're guided by a loving God who has welcomed you into His family. So we pray you will continue this journey and will strive to keep growing and learning as you seek to live a life that glorifies God.

REFLECTIVE QUESTIONS

Welcome to the reflective questions section of this book, designed to provide an opportunity for personal growth and deeper understanding as you embark on your Christian journey. These questions are meant to be pondered and processed in the quiet moments of reflection, allowing the Lord to work in your heart and mind.

It is important to approach these questions with a spirit of openness and receptiveness, understanding that personal growth is a gradual process. There is no rush, and there is no pressure to have all the answers. Each question is an invitation to delve deeper into your relationship with God and explore the truths presented in this book.

The intention behind these questions is not to burden you with more "should's," "got-to's," or "have to's." Rather, they are meant to serve as an encouragement, providing an opportunity for self-reflection and personal transformation. The Christian journey is a lifelong adventure, and these questions are tools to help you navigate and deepen your walk with the Lord.

As you engage with these questions, remember that the process itself is valuable. Take the time to truly reflect on each question, allowing the Holy Spirit to guide your thoughts and illuminate your understanding. Embrace the opportunity to grow, learn, and draw closer to God as you journey through these reflections.

May these questions be a source of inspiration, encouragement, and spiritual insight as you navigate the path of faith. Let them be a catalyst for meaningful conversations with God and a source of self-discovery. Remember, there is no right or wrong answer—what matters most is your willingness to engage and be transformed by the truth revealed.

Embrace this moment of reflection, let the Lord do the work within you, and trust that He is faithful to guide you on your unique Christian journey.

CHAPTER 1: THE CHRISTIAN LIFE

1. As you reflect on Jesus Christ's life, what characteristics stand out to you most and how can you strive to emulate these in your daily life?

2. What specific principles (like love, forgiveness, service, integrity) that Jesus taught do you believe you need to incorporate more in your life? How could you go about doing so?

3. Reflecting on the role of the Holy Spirit in your life, can you share an experience when you discerned the Holy Spirit guiding, empowering, or transforming you?

4. Can you identify a specific spiritual discipline (prayer, Bible study, worship, fasting, fellowship) that you feel you need to deepen or develop further? What steps could you take to grow in this area?

5. Despite the challenges and pressures of living a Christian life, in what ways have you experienced God's guidance and strength in your life? Can you share a moment when God's presence especially strongly during a difficult time?

CHAPTER 2: FAITH

1. Reflect on your understanding of faith. How would you describe your faith in God and Jesus Christ? How does this faith impact your daily thoughts, decisions, and interactions?

2. How do you respond to the idea that faith in Jesus is not about our works, but His? In your own journey, have you experienced struggles in accepting salvation as a gift rather than something to be earned?

3. Can you recall a specific instance when you have 'lived by faith, not by sight'? What did this look like in practical terms, and how did it strengthen your relationship with God?

4. Reflect on your faith growth journey. What specific practices or disciplines (prayer, fasting, Bible study, fellowship, obeying God's commands) have most significantly contributed to your faith growth, and how might you deepen these practices?

5. Doubts and uncertainties are a normal part of a faith journey. Can you share an experience where you faced doubt or uncertainty and how you sought help or clarification to strengthen your faith? How did this experience shape your understanding of faith and grace?

CHAPTER 3: PRAYER

1. Reflecting on the Lord's Prayer in Matthew 6:9-13, how does this prayer guide us in aligning our hearts and desires with God's will, rather than trying to change His mind? How does this understanding affect your approach to prayer?

2. In what ways has prayer transformed your own heart and mind to align more closely with God's will and purposes? Can you share any specific instances where prayer has led to personal transformation?

3. Considering the verse from James 4:3 about approaching prayer with right motives, how can you ensure that your prayers are not self-centered but truly aligned with seeking God's will?

4. Considering the different forms of prayer (praise, petition, intercession, confession, thanksgiving), which type do you find yourself leaning towards most often and why? How might incorporating other types of prayer deepen your relationship with God?

5. The chapter emphasizes that prayer is a relationship builder with God, not just a religious duty. How does this perspective shift your understanding of prayer, and how can you make prayer a more consistent part of your life.

6. How has understanding Jesus' practice of withdrawing to pray, as discussed in the chapter, inspired or challenged you to set aside specific times for prayer in your own life?

7. What are some obstacles you have faced in your prayer life and how have you overcome them? How does Romans 8:26 offer comfort or assurance in these times?

8 How does understanding prayer as an ongoing dialogue with God, for every moment of every day, change your perception of prayer and its role in your life?

9. As prayer is a journey, how have you seen your prayer life evolve as you've grown in your faith? In what areas do you wish to further grow or mature in your prayer life?

CHAPTER 4: LOVE AND FORGIVENESS

1. How does understanding the depth of God's love for you influence how you love and interact with others? In what ways can you practically demonstrate this kind of love to those around you?

2. Reflecting on the "greatest commandment" in Matthew 22:37-39, how do you actively love God with all your heart, soul, and mind, and your neighbor as yourself? Can you identify any areas where this could be improved?

3. How has your understanding and experience of God's forgiveness impacted your ability to forgive others? Can you recall a time when you found it challenging to forgive, and how you navigated through it?

4. God's forgiveness of our sins is complete and absolute. Do you find it easy or difficult to fully accept this forgiveness and why? How might fully accepting God's forgiveness affect your ability to forgive yourself and others?

5. Given the statement that "forgiveness is a journey, not a destination", where do you find yourself currently on this journey? Are there unresolved situations where forgiveness needs to be extended or sought? What steps can you take, with God's help, to progress on this journey?

CHAPTER 5: COMPASSION & SERVICE

1.   Reflecting on Jesus as our role model for compassion, how can we challenge ourselves to show empathy and love to those who are traditionally overlooked or outcast in our own communities, similar to the leper in Mark 1:40-41?

2.   What are some practical ways you can transform your feelings of compassion into acts of service within your local community, considering the examples given in the chapter?

3.   Jesus emphasized that no act of service is beneath us, as evidenced by His washing of His disciples' feet. How does this challenge your understanding of service, and in what ways might you embrace tasks you previously considered beneath you?

4.   Reflect on the statement, "When we serve others, we serve God." How does this concept influence your perspective on service, and what actions might you take in your life to better serve others and, in turn, God?

5.   In our modern, digital world, we are often more isolated despite being more connected. How can you use technology as a tool for expressing compassion and service in your interactions with others, and what challenges do you anticipate as you try to enact these virtues digitally?

CHAPTER 6: INTEGRITY

1. Reflect on Proverbs 10:9, *"Whoever walks in integrity walks securely, but whoever takes crooked paths will be found out."* How does this scripture speak to your understanding of the relationship between integrity and inner peace or security in your Christian walk?

2. Given that God is described as a God of integrity in Numbers 23:19, how does this influence your perception of God's character and what steps can you take to reflect His integrity in your own life?

3. Looking at Jesus as a model of integrity, particularly in His interactions with the Pharisees and in resisting temptation, how can you incorporate this level of truthfulness, righteousness, and consistency in your own life, both in public and private spheres?

4. Considering the biblical examples of Daniel and Joseph, in what ways have you faced tests of your own integrity, and how did you or could you respond to these challenges in a way that aligns with your Christian faith?

5. Ephesians 4:25 instructs us to speak truthfully and to avoid falsehood. How can you apply this in your daily life, particularly in your relationships, work, or school environment? Are there specific areas or situations where you need to focus on improving your honesty and truthfulness?

CHAPTER 7: RESPECT

1. How do you understand the biblical concept of respect, and in what ways can you consciously apply it in your daily interactions?

2. In light of the understanding of self-respect presented in this chapter, are there areas in your life where you may be disrespecting yourself, whether physically, emotionally, or spiritually? How can you address these areas in a manner that honors God's creation?

3. Respect for others can sometimes be challenging, especially when we encounter differences or disagreements. How can you maintain a posture of respect even when you fundamentally disagree with someone else's beliefs or actions?

4. Reflecting on your relationships with family, friends, and community, how does respect play out in these interactions? Are there relationships where you could improve the level of respect? If so, what practical steps can you take to increase respect in these relationships?

5. Respecting those in authority can be complex, especially when their directives contradict your understanding of God's commands. How can you balance the biblical call to respect authority while standing firm in your faith and convictions? Can you think of a situation where you might have to make such a decision, and how would you approach it respectfully?

CHAPTER 8: STEWARDSHIP

1. Reflect on the various areas of stewardship mentioned in this chapter (environment, body, talents, time, resources). Which area do you feel you've been stewarding well, and which area could use improvement?

2. The chapter mentions that stewardship isn't just about what we have, but also who has us. How does your understanding of belonging to God influence your approach to stewardship?

3. What practical steps can you take to improve your stewardship of the environment? Consider both small everyday habits and larger lifestyle changes.

4. How can you better steward your talents for God's glory? Are there talents you have that you might not be utilizing fully?

5. Stewardship of our time requires us to balance work, rest, service, and personal growth. How are you currently managing these aspects? What changes could you make to better steward your time according to biblical principles?

CHAPTER 9:GRATITUDE

1. How can you better recognize God's blessings in your daily life and express your gratitude for them?

2. Reflect on a difficult time you've experienced recently. How can you find reasons for gratitude in that situation, as suggested in Romans 5:3-5?

3. What steps can you take to cultivate a daily attitude of thankfulness, regardless of your circumstances, as discussed in Colossians 3:15-17 and Ephesians 5:20?

4. How can you more effectively show your gratitude to others around you, and what impact do you think this could have on your relationship with them and with God?

5. In the practice of keeping a gratitude journal, what specific things have you found yourself most thankful for, and how does acknowledging these blessings improve your relationship with God?

CHAPTER 10: PATIENCE & PERSEVERANCE

1. Reflect on a recent difficult situation in your life. How did the virtues of patience and perseverance manifest themselves during this time, and how did they help you endure this hardship? How can you cultivate these qualities further?

2. As discussed in this chapter, understanding and accepting God's timing can be challenging. Can you share a time when God's timeline differed from yours? How did this test your patience and what did you learn from this experience?

3. The chapter discusses the importance of being patient with others and ourselves. Can you recall an instance where you struggled to be patient with yourself or someone else? What steps can you take to improve your patience in these areas?

4. Job's story is one of great perseverance in the face of immense suffering. How does his story inspire you in your personal struggles? How can you apply the lessons from Job's experience in your life?

5. Romans 5:3-5 discusses the role of suffering in developing perseverance and character. Can you share a personal experience where a difficult situation led to growth in your character or faith? How can you encourage others going through similar circumstances to view their challenges as opportunities for growth rather than mere suffering?

CHAPTER 11: COMMUNITY AND FELLOWSHIP

1. Reflecting on Community and Fellowship: The book of Acts presents the early Christian community as a model of mutual love, shared faith, and collective worship. How do you personally contribute to these aspects in your Christian community? Can you identify any areas where you could contribute more?

2. Practicing Benefits of Christian Community: Proverbs 27:17 says, *"As iron sharpens iron, so one person sharpens another."* How have you experienced this sharpening in your community? Can you share an example of a time when someone in your community has helped you grow spiritually?

3. Understanding the Role of Fellowship: Fellowship involves sharing life experiences, spiritual insights, and our love for God. How can you deepen your involvement in fellowship? What steps can you take to more regularly share your spiritual insights and experiences with others?

4. Strengthening Church Relationships: Building strong relationships within the church requires intentional effort and regular participation in church activities. How might you become more involved in your church's activities or small groups? Are there ways you can serve others within your community to strengthen these bonds?

5. Navigating Challenges and Playing a Role in the Global Church: As you face challenges in your community, how can you apply the biblical principles of reconciliation and forgiveness from Matthew 18:15-17 and Ephesians 4:32? Considering your role in the global Church, how might you support fellow believers who are persecuted or in need, either through prayer or practical means?

CHAPTER 12: HUMILITY

1. How does our understanding of humility shift when we see it as "thinking of ourselves less and of others and God more" instead of seeing it as a form of self-deprecation or low self-esteem?

2. Reflecting on Jesus' examples of humility, such as washing the feet of His disciples and His crucifixion, how can we apply these examples in our own lives and relationships? What might foot washing or sacrificial humility look like in your day-to-day interactions?

3. Considering the importance of humility in Christian life, in what ways can you see humility as a "soil in which other virtues grow"? How does it influence your ability to be teachable, patient, forgiving, and compassionate?

4. In what ways can you practically cultivate humility in your life? Using the methods mentioned in this chapter, such as self-reflection, service, gratitude, empathy, and prayer, create a plan for how you will integrate these into your life.

5. Reflect on the role of humility in your relationships and any leadership roles you hold. How does your understanding of humility influence how you interact with others, make decisions, and serve those around you?

CHAPTER 13: HOPE AND JOY

1. How does the biblical understanding of hope, as a confident expectation rather than just wishful thinking, shape your approach to future challenges and uncertainties?

2. In what ways have you experienced the deep, unshakeable joy that comes from knowing God, even in times of difficulty or pain? Can you share an example?

3. Romans 15:13 highlights God as the source of our hope and joy. How does regularly focusing on God's character and promises help you maintain hope and joy in your daily life?

4. Practicing gratitude is suggested as one practical way to cultivate hope and joy. Can you identify specific instances in your life right now for which you're thankful, and explain how this practice uplifts your spirit?

5. Maintaining hope and joy is a lifelong journey that requires persistence, patience, and continual reliance on God. Can you share a situation where your hope and joy were tested, and how you sought God's assistance in maintaining these virtues?

CHAPTER 14: BIBLE STUDY

1. What specific steps can you take to improve the consistency of your Bible study, considering the distractions and busyness of everyday life?

2. How does inviting the Holy Spirit into your time of reading and reflection change the experience of your Bible study?

3. The chapter emphasizes the importance of understanding what the author was saying to the original audience when studying the Bible. Can you share an example where this approach altered your understanding or application of a certain passage?

4. Considering the various Bible study techniques mentioned (SOAP Method, Inductive Bible Study, Verse Mapping, Topical Study), which one are you most drawn to and why? How could this method help deepen your understanding of God's Word?

5. How can you apply what you've learned from your Bible study into your everyday life? Can you share a specific instance where your understanding of a scripture passage led to a change in your behavior, attitude, or perspective?

CHAPTER 15: WHITNESSING & SHARING THE GOSPEL

1. The Importance of Authenticity: It's essential to be honest and authentic when sharing your faith. People are more likely to engage with a message that comes from a genuine place. It's okay to admit that you don't have all the answers and that you're still growing in your faith.

2. Praying for Opportunities: Regularly ask God for opportunities to share your faith. Pray for open doors and the ability to notice when someone is open and ready to hear the Gospel.

3. Praying for those you're witnessing to: In addition to praying for opportunities to witness, it's essential to pray for the people you're witnessing to. Ask God to work in their hearts and open their eyes to the truth of the Gospel.

4. Don't be discouraged by rejection: It's important to remember that you're not responsible for how people respond to the Gospel. If someone rejects the message, don't take it personally. Remember that it's God who changes hearts, not us.

5. Trust in God's timing: God works according to His own perfect timeline. Sometimes, the seeds you plant through witnessing may take a long time to bear fruit. Be patient and trust that God is at work, even when you can't see it.

6. Fellowship with other believers: Sharing your faith can feel daunting, but you don't have to do it alone. Surrounding yourself with other believers can provide you with support, encouragement, and advice.

CHAPTER 16: LIVING A CHRIST-CENTERED LIFE

1. Reflecting on Galatians 2:20, what steps can you take to ensure that Christ is the central figure in your everyday decisions and interactions? How can you live out the principle of Christ living in you more fully?

2. Based on the impact of a Christ-centered life outlined in the chapter, in what ways have you experienced personal transformation since you began your journey with Christ? How have you seen your actions and attitudes influence those around you?

3. With the practical ways to live a Christ-centered life in mind, how can you strengthen your spiritual disciplines such as prayer and Bible study? What specific steps will you take this week to serve others, share the gospel, and foster community and fellowship?

4. Romans 10:9 emphasizes the importance of confessing with our mouths that Jesus is Lord and believing in our hearts that God raised him from the dead. Reflecting on this, what does it mean to you personally to trust in Jesus as your Lord and Savior?

5. It is noted that challenges and doubts are part of the journey of living a Christ-centered life. Can you recall a time when you faced a challenge or doubt in your faith? How did you rely on God during that time? In retrospect, how did that experience help you grow in your faith and deepen your understanding of God?

www.ingramcontent.com/pod-product-compliance
Lightning Source LLC
La Vergne TN
LVHW021516080426
835509LV00018B/2530